THE
TRIBULATION
STRATEGY

FAITH IN THE COMING STORM

SAMUEL B. BLACK

WestBow
PRESS

WestBow Press books may be ordered through booksellers or by contacting:

WestBow Press
A Division of Thomas Nelson
1663 Liberty Drive
Bloomington, IN 47403
www.westbowpress.com
1-(866) 928-1240

Because of the dynamic nature of the Internet, any Web addresses or links contained in this book may have changed since publication and may no longer be valid. The views expressed in this work are solely those of the author and do not necessarily reflect the views of the publisher, and the publisher hereby disclaims any responsibility for them.

ISBN: 978-1-4497-0298-4 (sc)
ISBN: 978-1-4497-0299-1 (hc)
ISBN: 978-1-4497-0297-7 (e)

Library of Congress Control Number: 2010931003

Printed in the United States of America

WestBow Press rev. date: 7/19/2010

ACKNOWLEDGMENTS

I would like to thank my family for being so supportive while *The Tribulation Strategy: Faith in the Coming Storm* was written. I would also like to convey special thanks to my brother. He helped strengthen my faith through sincere fellowship while I endured several significant hardships. During those hardships God revealed the message of this book to me.

Samuel Black
JANUARY 2010

CONTENTS

Acknowledgments v

Preface ix

Introduction xi

1. Major Viewpoints Discussed 1

2. Missed Warnings 17

3. The Critique and the Package 23

4. Unveiling the Unholy Trinity 27

5. Daniel 9:25–27 Discussed 33

6. The Hasty Advent 39

7. Hell the Lamb 45

8. The Image of Abomination 51

9. The Broken Covenant 59

10. Faith in the Coming Storm 67

Appendix A: Affirmation Of Faith 73

Appendix B: The First And Second Damnation 79

Appendix C: Can Christians Judge? 81

Selected Bibliography 85

Notes 87

PREFACE

It is my sincere hope that readers will consider the messages contained in this book, without biases toward denominations or loyalties to previous teachings. It is our humble duty as Christians to discuss and scrutinize doctrines for correctness and truth. We cannot deny errors and discrepancies to save face.

In my opinion, many Christians have set themselves up for a fall. They have accepted deceptive doctrines that were skillfully joined together with words of truth. The Lord warned, "many shall come in my name, saying, I am Christ; and shall deceive many" (Matt. 24:5). Christians come in the name of the Lord. Therefore, according to the Lord's warning, certain well-known Christian teachings are spreading deception on a large scale. This book was written, in part, to shed light on that deception. It will also demonstrate methods for identifying and understanding apocalyptic texts.

Apocalyptic texts are important because they are laden with warnings that God intended for the last generations of his Church to heed. Related to those warnings are important teachings strewn throughout Scripture that Christians often overlook.

As God reveals his plans for the end, some may find them troubling: "For in much wisdom is much grief: and he that increaseth knowledge increaseth sorrow" (Eccl. 1:18). Without question, apocalyptic texts contain horrible events that humanity has never seen (cf. Matt. 24:21). Those events may leave the unsaved and unfaithful with feelings of hopelessness and fear. We, however, have comfort in knowing that when they pass, the Lord will wipe every tear from our eyes (Rev. 7:17). That is our hope.

God did not give us apocalyptic information that we might never understand. John wrote, "Blessed is he that readeth, and they that hear the words of this prophecy" (Rev. 1:3). What powerful words! The Apocalypse and all related writings were meant for you.

INTRODUCTION

To begin, many teachings on the tribulation focus on what will happen, but never really answer why they will happen. This leaves Christians open to future attacks on their faith designed to create doubt. Make no mistake; those spiritual attacks have already started. In the future, however, Satan will orchestrate these attacks with increasing hostility and cunning application. This is why Christians must equip themselves, even now, with an understanding of why those future events will take place. The result of that exploration reveals the tribulation's true purpose—one that relates to faith.

Faith is a relative term. Someone who says he or she has faith may not be referring necessarily to faith in Christianity. In fact, he or she may be faithful to other gods or religious systems. Therefore, faith is simply the loyal belief in something. Within Christianity, faith is the loyal belief in the death, burial, and resurrection of the Lord Jesus Christ. He gave his life to redeem all people who truly believe in him and what he accomplished at the cross (cf. John 3:16, Heb. 9:28). That should be the basis for all Christian faith, because without it there is no hope. That is why Christian faith is the gift of hope.

Christians receive that gift from the Holy Spirit (1 Cor. 12:7–9). Like other gifts from the Spirit, faith serves both spiritual and natural purposes. The gift of healing, for example, confirmed to observers the divine presence of the Holy Spirit. It also provided much needed relief to the natural bodies of those who were healed.

The gift of diverse tongues (languages) also confirmed the presence of the Holy Spirit and ensured that the Church would preach the gospel in foreign lands. Therefore, its natural purpose was to remove the hindrances of language barriers to facilitate the spreading gospel. Those who witnessed that miraculous translation, and heard the gospel of salvation, confirmed the workings of the Spirit (Acts 2:6–33).

The gift of faith is no different. Its spiritual purpose is to confirm the presence of the Holy Spirit. Its natural purpose is to enable Christians to persevere through a wide variety of difficulties. During those difficulties, they can turn toward God and rely on their faith when all else fails. For that reason, it is an essential part of Christian life.

Ministers of Light

Unfortunately, some corrupt leaders demonstrate or imitate the gifts of the Spirit to gain the trust of observing Christians (Matt. 7:15, 10:16, Luke 10:3). In positions of trust, those corrupt leaders can easily exploit their congregations (2 Pet. 2:1–3). That is why it is necessary to scrutinize the spiritual and natural purposes of a gift in order to determine the validity of its manifestation. If one cannot determine a dual purpose, then the possibility of deception is there.

Consider how the gospel of Christ is now known around the world (Matt. 24:14). It was not only conveyed through speech, but also through the native written languages of many nations. God's translators and missionaries did their jobs well. That is why the Holy Spirit no longer grants the gift of diverse earthly tongues (1 Cor. 13:8). What natural purpose would it serve in this current age?

In regards to angelic (unknown) tongues, Paul wrote that he would rather speak words that were easily understood than speak an unknown language that benefited no one; his point being that there must be a spiritual and natural purpose to the exercise of a gift.[1] Speaking angelic tongues in public only serves a spiritual purpose, so observers are not edified in their natural minds. Why? Because without interpretation, they hear only unrecognizable sounds (cf. 1 Cor. 14:23, 14:27–28). That is not to say that there is something wrong with that gift. It is simply a matter of how it is sometimes used.

In private settings, or even in public settings with an interpreter present, speaking an angelic language may be an enriching experience. However, when it is purposefully demonstrated for show, it serves no other purpose than to "spiritually boast." It is very much like the hypocrites, who broadcasted their religious activities so they would be looked upon as holy (Matt. 6:1–8).

Using any gift without purpose is self-serving (1 Cor. 14:4–12), and using any gift for "spiritual boasting" is abuse. That is why the motives of anyone claiming to have spiritual gifts should be questioned if their demonstration of gifts falls into any of those categories.

The Lord warned centuries ago that Satan and his ministers would appear as light (2 Cor. 11:13–15). Light is symbolic of righteousness and hope. Considering that 2 Corinthians was written for the Church, it is clear that God directed a warning at Christians. He wanted them to be aware that Satan's ministers would appear as righteous ministers of hope and truth. God does not lie, so those ministers are here now, preaching to the masses false words mingled with truth (2 Pet. 2:1). Can they be identified? Are their locations known? Those ministers of light were here during the infancy of the Church and they will be here in the end, continuing to deceive many people.

With that in mind, consider the complaints of a select group of people condemned to the lake of fire (Matt. 7:21–23). Notice how they disputed their damnation by telling God that they wielded the gifts of the Spirit. They demonstrated the gifts of prophesy, cast out demons, and performed miraculous works in the Lord's name (cf. Matt. 24:5, Mark 16:17, 1 Cor. 12:8–10).[2] Those people were so convinced they were saved that they argued about their fate (Matt. 8:12).

With that account of his coming judgment, the Lord emphasized that the ability to demonstrate spiritual gifts is not always a sign of righteousness and salvation. Those people, before his throne, are fallen Christians (cf. 1 Tim. 4:1). They focused more on empty promises and spiritual gifts than on the death, burial, and resurrection of Jesus Christ. They lost sight of what was most important. For that reason, when their faith was covertly tested, they failed.

That test, as well as how Christians can lose their salvation, will be in the subject matter of later chapters. For now, the discerning Christian benefits from knowing that not everyone who claims to have spiritual gifts can be trusted. In fact, some are frauds. Faithful Christians will know them, not only by their works, but also by their abuse and/or imitation of spiritual gifts.

Identifying them is important because they prey on the innocent. How many times have skeptics uncovered scandal and trickery in Christian churches? Some of those incidents were highly publicized.[3] Many of those ungodly ministers, teachers, and self-proclaimed prophets tricked their congregations into believing they were powerful people of God (cf. Deut.

13, 18:20, Jer. 14:15). Some appeared credible because they demonstrated something that looked like spiritual gifts (cf. 2 Cor. 11:14). Others appeared credible because they occupied respectable positions within their churches.

Corrupted leaders claim to represent God, but are not from God. For that reason, edifying the Church is not their priority. Their motivation is greed. The warning in 2 Peter 2:3 goes so far as to say that they will "make merchandise of you." They pursue greed with reckless abandon. They will preach anything a congregation wants to hear to win favor and trust, without considering the consequences of their deceitful teachings and frauds. They exploit the weak in faith by offering false hopes during hardships. They speak prophecies that do not come true. They promise prosperity that never comes to fruition. They even claim to heal sick people, but these people still suffer after their "healings." They do all of those deceitful things, in God's name, for purposes of greed.

Their transgressions have caused many people to experience disappointments. Those disappointments are then blamed on God. In their minds, God is the one who failed to deliver on his promises. But, there is the twist. God did not make those promises. Satan's ministers of light made them. That is the truth about their light. It is false hope.

Poorly Rooted Faith

Unfortunately, many of the people who follow ministers of light also demonstrate the true conditions of their faith. Their faith was never based on the accomplishments of Jesus Christ at the cross. Instead, it was based on false expectations. Their corrupted leaders wrongly conditioned them to expect only good things in this life. For that reason, they were not mentally prepared for the hardships and realities of Christian life in this ungodly world.

In Matthew 13:5–6 that type of poorly rooted faith is symbolized as seeds that fell on stony places. Those seeds, unlike the seeds in verse 4, had some faith. That is why they were able to sprout roots. It was the depth of those roots that turned out to be insufficient when tested by the sun (Matt. 13:20–21). Another way of looking at it would be to say that their poorly rooted faith failed when tested by tribulation. It is also interesting to note that the end product is offense (verse 21). They were so offended that their Christian faith did not exempt them from the "heat" of the tribulation that they turned away. That same response is observed again in Matthew 24:10.

False Expectations

It is important to know that it is not too late for many people to leave those false ministries and rededicate their lives to Jesus Christ. To do that they will need to properly root their faith in his resurrection. They will also have to understand that tribulations are a part of Christian life. Even great people in the Bible had to endure tribulations.

The apostle Paul, for example, was confined to a prison for preaching the resurrection. To make matters worse, he was abandoned by his friends. Those events were so trying that they left him feeling lonely and depressed (cf. 2 Tim. 1:8–15, 4:9–16). That is why those negative feelings set the overall tone for his writings in 2 Timothy. Are Christians in this current age any closer to God than Paul?

Christian teachings that create false expectations leave many believers confused when unfortunate events occur. While confused, they are further disheartened because their turmoil is often blamed on sin. In other words, they must have done something wrong to incur the wrath of God. If not, their lives would be filled with blessings and bliss. The Bible, however, teaches a much different lesson.

That lesson is that hardships cannot always be blamed on the backslidden or spiritually weakened states of Christians. In fact, the Lord warned that his followers would be hated, persecuted, and, in many cases, martyred just for having faith in him (Matt. 10:22, 24:9). Christians, who suffer tribulations for their faith, are an enigma to those who do not understand. Job's friends, for example, blamed his tribulation on unconfessed sin (Job 5). The truth of the matter was that Job was a righteous man being tested by God (Job 1:8–12).

People should never be taught to expect an easy and prosperous life in this world as a result of their acceptance of Jesus Christ (cf. 1 Tim. 6:6–7). Likewise, they should not associate worldly things, like prosperity, with righteousness and salvation. If one Christian is rich and another poor, so be it. Their faith and relationship to God have very little to do with their social status or worldly possessions. In fact, all Christians are spiritually equal. Paul addressed such an issue in his letter to Philemon.

His reason for writing the letter was to reconcile a runaway slave, Onesimus, with his owner. Paul let Philemon know that his runaway slave was now a brother in faith (Philem. 1:16). He later asked Philemon to receive Onesimus as a partner (verse 17). With those words, Paul changed Philemon's worldly view into a spiritual view. Onesimus was now equal to his owner in the eyes of the Lord (cf. Rom. 15:6–7).

The same holds true for unfortunate events. The fortunate are no closer to God than the unfortunate (cf. Matt. 5:45). Take for example a child who is born blind. Blindness is one of the many unfortunate manifestations of original sin. The child did nothing wrong. In fact, the curse he bares stems from a sin he did not commit. Should a child born with sight be looked upon as more righteous? Just because original sin manifested itself as blindness in one and not the other does not indicate a superior spiritual state. In fact, original sin may have manifested itself much differently in the child with sight. Blindness, for lack of better words, was a random and unfortunate event.

Focusing on Faith

Make no mistake; there are times when God will punish for sin. Scripture makes that quite clear. The problem is making a distinction between a tribulation for sin and a tribulation for faith. Often times, that distinction cannot be made. For that reason, it is important to approach any Christian, who is suffering through a tribulation, with the primary intent of strengthening his or her faith.

Recall for a moment the storm that almost capsized the boat carrying Jesus Christ and the apostles (Mark 4:37–40). That storm was a tribulation. Notice what Jesus said after he rebuked the wind and sea: "How is it that ye have no faith" (verse 40). He was not interested in the storm at all. He was more concerned about the apostle's lack of faith. The irony of the situation was that the apostles were in a boat, with the Creator of all things, and feared a mere storm (cf. 2 Tim. 1:7). Likewise, many Christians falter during their own personal "storms." Their improper reactions are directly related to the conditions of their faith.

Think how an ice cream cone reacts as it is exposed to heat. The ice cream melts away quickly, leaving behind an empty cone. Now consider how a piece of metal reacts to even greater heat: the greater the heat, the more it is purified. Ice cream represents weak faith and the metal represents strong faith. Heat is symbolic of tribulation. Therefore, the initial condition of a Christian's faith determines how he or she will react to the "heat" of tribulation.[4] That is why the Church should continually seek to strengthen the faith of its members (Gala. 6:1–2).

If the root cause of a tribulation is sin, strengthening a Christian's faith, with prayer, help, and hope, will do much more than chastisement. If the root cause of a tribulation is faith, providing a Christian with the prayers and hope necessary to see past the turmoil will result in a stronger, more faithful, and proven servant of the Lord.

Having said that, it is important to understand that sometimes tribulations for faith are just the beginnings of better things to come. Job was given an increase of everything he lost. God rewarded him because he endured his suffering to the end and his faith never changed (cf. Matt. 5:11–12). At times, God wants his people to demonstrate that they are trustworthy and ready for greater blessings (cf. Luke 16:10, James 2:5, John 14:2).

***

Without the strength and support of fellow Christians, many who are dealing with tribulations will doubt their faith. Doubt stems from a lack of understanding. If they do not understand the causes of their tribulations they may feel abandoned or unfairly punished. They may even question God's authority or existence. Without question, doubt is a critical stumbling block. It is also the beginning of the falling away process mentioned in 2 Thessalonians 2:3 and 1 Timothy 4:1.

That is why the first step in understanding the end time tribulation is to understand its purpose. Without that understanding, many will doubt their faith during that difficult time. Their doubts will stem, in part, from the confusing events that will unfold. To add to their dilemma, God revealed that he would be the authority behind those events (2 Thess. 2:11). Fortunately, for the faithful Church, he revealed his reasons for causing that confusion in certain parables (cf. Matt. 13:10–17, 13:35).

Tares and Wheat

One such parable is found in Matthew 13:24–50. As with other parables, symbolism is used in the beginning, but a complete interpretation and explanation is given at the end. That is how readers know what the symbolism means. In this case, the field is the world, the seeds are the Church, tares (weeds) are infiltrators of that Church, and the harvest is the end of this age, when God will send his angels to remove his Church from this world (verses 38, 39, 41).

This parable is sometimes interpreted to mean the separation of believers from unbeliever, but read carefully and notice who seeded in the field. It was the Son of Man. He is the one who planted the Church. The members of that Church are the children of his kingdom. This parable is not describing the creation of humankind. If it did, Satan would have to be credited with planting at least some life here on earth. Why? Because he planted seeds too (Matt. 13:39). That is clearly not the case (John 1:1–3). The beginning of this parable describes the planting of the Christian Church, in this world, by Jesus Christ.

Now notice how the weeds were planted among the wheat (cf. Acts 20:29–31, 2 Pet. 2:1–9). They were blended into the Church around the same time it was planted. That is why the corruption they introduced grew within the Church. It was God's choice to allow them to grow because the harvest would be the best time to remove them (verse 30). His reasons for that delay will become clearer in later chapters. For now, know that from the time of the Church's inception to now, there has been an ongoing spiritual battle between "wheat" and "weeds."

Think how many times the apostles had to "clean house" by refuting the false doctrines and misrepresentations made by Church infiltrators. One of the more notable occasions occurred in 2 Corinthians 11:13–15, when Paul issued a warning about false apostles masquerading as real apostles. Imagine the corrupted doctrines they introduced. Now, imagine the multitude of other doctrines introduced by other infiltrators from Paul's time to now (cf. 1 Tim. 1).[5] Those infiltrators were not "planted" by God, and for that reason never belonged (Matt. 15:13). True followers of Christ would never devise such devious plans.

God is aware of them. He knows that they called his name only to achieve their wicked purposes (cf. Acts 2:21, Matt. 7:21). They were warned of the damnation that would follow anyone who became a part of his blood covenant with ulterior motives (1 Cor. 11:27–29). That is why God will not allow them to be saved with his Church.

Those infiltrators grew with the Church, but are not part of the Church. The same goes for those who continue to follow them (Matt. 15:14). Weeds do not make good crops. For that reason, God will root them out one by one (Matt. 13:28–30, 13:37–43). In the future, they will be severed from the blood covenant. God will "gather out of *his* kingdom all things that offend" (Matt. 13:41). That is the primary purpose of the end time tribulation. It is a separation process within the Church.

For comparison, notice how God used the term "evil servant" in Matthew 24:48. That parable warns of the unexpected time the Lord will return (verse 42). It also describes the behavior of the servants he made rulers of his household. That symbolic household is a clear reference to his earthly Church, because it requires the governance and stewardship of his servants (cf. 1 Tim. 3:5, Gala. 6:10, Matt. 24:43, Eph. 2:19). Those who remain "faithful and wise" will later rule over all of his "goods" (verses 45–47). Goods are symbolic of greater things to come.

Later, in that same parable, a servant is found abusing his position (verse 48–51). He turned on his fellow servants for personal gratification and gain. That turning process revealed his true nature. It relates directly to how the weeds will appear before the harvest (Matt. 13:26). We know that the evil servant symbolizes corrupt members of the Church because the Lord would not appoint unbelievers to rule his "household" or "goods" (cf. Mark 13:34–37). Those corrupt members are the ones who gnashed teeth (quarreled) and wept after learning about their fate (Matt. 7:22, 13:49–50, 22:13, 24:51).

Job

Besides parables, God used parallels to convey insight to his Church. Parallels are passages in Scripture that teach valuable lessons using indirect references to other events. They are similar but at the same time different. The similarities teach the lessons. Often times, those lessons are repeated to place emphasis and confirmation on divine orchestration.

Notice the parallel between the account of Moses lifting up a serpent in the wilderness and Jesus being lifted up on the cross (Num. 21:7–9, John 3:14–15). Both events resulted in a select group of people being saved from a horrible fate. Another parallel can be drawn from the three days Jonah stayed in the belly of a large fish and the time Jesus spent in the earth (Jon. 1:17, Matt. 12:40). The Lord recounted Jonah's ordeal because only God can create parallels of time generations apart.

Some parallels are not as easy to identify as those mentioned above, especially when they are not mentioned directly or explained. The story of Job and his suffering is one such parallel. It sets an important precedence for a later period of tribulation that will be observed on a much larger scale.

Interestingly enough, you must first understand the story of Job in order to understand how God intends to root out the "weeds" from his Church.

The scenario itself is insightful, because much like many apocalyptic passages, events are happening in heaven and on earth. Readers are given a look into the happenings of the higher realm. They see how the principalities and authorities of heaven sometimes consider and test the hearts of men (cf. Eph. 3:10, 6:12). They also see, first hand, the wicked mindset of someone the Lord described as an accuser (John 5:45). In Job, we see first hand how that accuser operates.

As Satan appeared before God, he provided a mischievous answer to the inquiry about where he had been. He said, in so many words, that he had been busy on the earth. Most likely, his actions there had something to do with God's next question: "Hast thou considered my servant Job" (Job 1:8)? Based on that question, one can infer that Satan was considering and accusing people on the earth. He was pointing out failure—but failure of what? What were his accusations?

Based on his response, and the context of the conversation, the obvious answer was hypocrisy. Satan was demonstrating to God the failure and hypocrisy of peoples' faith. His accusations were insightful because they also revealed his targets. He would not accuse nonbelievers of hypocrisy, because they have no faith in the first place. His target group was, and still is, God's people.

Satan must have exposed a great deal of hypocrisy for God to feel the need to point out someone who was not so easily swayed. Job was not like those other people. God said, "there is none like him in the earth" (Job 1:8). Something about Job made him stand out. The fact that God knew him also demonstrated his omnipresence.

God knows his people. He knows how they act in public and how they act behind closed doors. He is not fooled by Sunday morning good behavior. He is always watching to see if the people who called his name did what he told them to do. Have they forgiven the trespasses of all people, or is hatred and vengeance still found in their hearts (cf. Matt. 18:23–35, 6:12–15)? Do they view all believers in Christ as spiritual equals, or do they judge based on race and status (Rom. 15:5–7)? Are they faithful to him no matter what happens around them, or is their faith easily swayed? God knows his faithful servants. He also knows each and every hypocrite in his Church. It is a grievous misunderstanding to think that he will tolerate such behavior.[6]

Job's Example

Now, notice how Satan did not provide any positive information about humanity, even when asked about Job. What he should have said was that his attempts to expose Job as a hypocrite had failed. How else would he have known about his divine protection and blessings unless, at some point, he came against them (Job 1:10)? His hatred for humanity prevented him from making that admission. Instead, he asserted that Job was only faithful because he had an easy and prosperous life. He wanted to demonstrate that if Job's situation were changed, for the worse, his faith would fade away; but, as stated before, God knows his people.

By choosing Job for the test, God provided the Church with one of the best examples of what a relationship with him should entail. He allowed Job to be tested at the hands of Satan in order to reveal the true faith of one of his servants. No matter how much he suffered, Job never changed his reverence, respect, or love for God. His relationship transcended his physical state. It did not matter how high or low he was, he always kept his faith. In using Job as an example, God set the standard high for his people (James 5:10–11).

Job's faith allowed him to persevere through the confusion, pain, and suffering. Ungodly words from friends and family did not sway him. He stood by his faith even when confronted with false accusations of sin. Recall that even Jesus was accused of evil (Matt. 10:25, 12:24–30). Job demonstrated to his accuser, that there are those on this earth who have true faith in God.

Job's test was a blueprint for a greater test to come. It also demonstrated the method for passing that test. That method is to live by undying and unchanging faith. When those "weeds" fall away, it will be because they lose faith. Job had nothing but his faith by the time Satan was finished ruining his life. He could not affect his surroundings or make people understand. He could not even rely on his friends. All he had was his reverence for God.

God not only used Job's suffering to demonstrate true faith; he also used it to root out the "weeds" that were positioned around Job (as they are in and around the Church). Think how he chastised Job's friends when the test was over (Job 42:7–8). What could they say? They were not even aware that he was watching and listening. Job was the one who suffered, but they were exposed as "weeds." God knows who is true to him and he knows who is not.

Some Christians love God only during easy times. When something goes wrong, their faith is easily broken. For that reason, each and every Christian should take time to reflect on their relationship with God and remember Job's example. That relationship is what will be tested in the Great Tribulation. As you will see, it is a test of faith (cf. 1 Pet. 1:3–9). Those who lose faith during that time will be exposed, led away, and separated from the Church. Those who keep their faith will be revealed as the righteous and shine in the glory of the Lord (Matt. 13:43).

NOTES

1. Paul's statement in 1 Corinthians 13:1 indicates that there are both earthly (known) and angelic (unknown) languages.

2. Also consult Titus 1:10–16 and note that those people are part of the circumcision and profess to know God. The people who are a part of the circumcision are defined in Philip 3:3.

3. A World Wide Web search using words like "Christian Ponzi Scheme" or "church fraud" will demonstrate not only the frequency of faith-based scams, but also their evolution as they adapt to defeat the legal system. One of the more notable cases involved Greater Ministries International Church, where the ranking ministers of that church were sentenced to lengthy prison terms for defrauding millions of dollars from their supporters.

    http://www.asc.state.al.us/News/PR-GRTERMINISTRIES 3-13-01.htm

    http://www.christianitytoday.com/ct/2001/october1/15.21.html

4. 1 Corinthians 3:10–15 teaches that even the works of men are scrutinized and tested to expose truth or hypocrisy (cf. Matt. 6:1–7).

5. Notice how they pursue positions of leadership and authority that afford them the ability to mislead with instruction.

6. In Matthew 7:21, the Lord's warning to do the will of his Father instead of just calling his name has far reaching implications.

1. MAJOR VIEWPOINTS DISCUSSED

Many denominations of the Christian faith have interpreted the millennial reign of Christ using one of the more major viewpoints (approaches). Each of those viewpoints can be substantiated to some degree. There are also four more viewpoints used for understanding the Apocalypse. To be clear, the Apocalypse encompasses a vast span of time that includes the Great Tribulation and millennial reign of Christ.

The purpose of this chapter is to discuss some of the strengths and weaknesses of those major viewpoints, in order to better understand the origins of current interpretations. It is important to know their roots, because many have been introduced as authoritative doctrines within the Church. Can they all be correct?

Amillennial Viewpoint

Basic Premises:

Amillennialism was developed by Augustine within the Alexandrian school of thought.[1] Augustine found objection to the "carnal way some premillennialists were describing life in the millennial kingdom."[2] In that respect, he may not have considered the state of mankind prior to Original Sin. It was perfect, not carnal. God provided everything in abundance, and his perfect creation (humanity) enjoyed those provisions. Only after Original Sin did carnality enter into the world.

A common misconception about amillennial teaching is that it does not allow for the literal interpretation of Revelation 20. The name itself adds to that misconception because "a" means "no."[3] So, in essence, the word means "no millennium," which clearly contradicts the amillennialist viewpoint.[4] In actuality, the amillennialist viewpoint does accept a literal reign of Christ. It is how they interpret that reign that sparks debate.

Amillennialists believe that the millennial reign began with the incarnation of Christ on Earth. Various biblical texts can be found to support that position (e.g. Matt. 16:28, Luke 17:20–21). They also believe that during the incarnation of Christ, Satan was curtailed from interfering with the spreading gospel, which is based, for the most part, on Revelation 20:2.[5] That curtailment is equated to binding, but only in regards to his ability to affect or prevail against the gospel.[6] In other respects, he is still allowed to continue his evil deeds.[7]

Points of Strength:

The amillennialist viewpoint presents a difficult interpretation to dispute because it is based on strong scriptural evidence. In some cases, the amillennialist interpretation of the text is also inline with other viewpoints. Even premillennialists can find supporting Scripture for the belief that believers have "risen with Christ" (Col. 3:1). That being said, there are significant problems with this viewpoint. The first is that the present state of Satan is in question. The second is that the timing of the second advent is debatable.

Points of Weakness:

The binding of Satan is an integral part of the amillennialist viewpoint, since it had to have happened for this present age to be considered the millennium. Therefore, if it were proven that he was not yet bound, one would have to look to the future for the fulfillment of that event. That also presents a problem to those who believe that the gospel is currently unhindered.

With that in mind, consider 2 Corinthians 4:3, where Paul speaks of a hidden gospel and later warns "the god of this world hath blinded the minds of them which believe not, lest the light of the glorious gospel of Christ, who is the image of God, should shine unto them" (2 Cor. 4:4). From that passage, one can infer that Satan is not yet bound. If he were, why would Paul make such a statement? In fact, Satan was able to tempt Jesus Christ (Matt. 4:1–10, Mark 1:13, Luke 4:2).[8] That act alone demonstrated that he was not only free, but also powerful enough to confront the living Word of God.

It is important to understand that evil spirits are subject to the authority of God's name, but for the most part those related texts deal with people tormented by demons, not the prevention of the spreading gospel. The Lord even warned that those spirits could return in greater force (cf. Matt. 12:43–45, Luke 11:24–26, Mark 5).

Now if the binding of Satan has not yet occurred, and it directly coincides with the millennial reign, one must ask if that too is a future event. If the millennial reign is a future event, then, according to the text, there has to be some specified time when the nations are no longer deceived before the final upheaval and white throne judgment (Rev. 20:3, 20:7–15).

That future period in time is in–line with another prophecy found in Daniel, where he saw the beast removed from authority but his subordinate kings allowed to live for a specific period of time (Dan. 7:12). That means that nations will still be allowed to exist in a natural state during the millennial reign of Christ (cf. Isa. 65:17–25). In sharp contrast, the resurrected saints will be made immortal kings and priests to reign with Christ over those fallen nations (cf. Rev. 2:26–27, 12:5, 19:15, Psalm 2).

Post-millennial Viewpoint

Basic Premises:

The post-millennial viewpoint is based on the premise that Jesus Christ will return "after a one-thousand-year period [of bliss]."[9] That period of bliss is believed to be the end result of the spreading gospel, which they liken to the rider of the white horse in Revelation 19.[10]

The post-millennial viewpoint is comparable to that of the amillennialist viewpoint in that they both believe the millennium reign does not involve the literal and visible presence of Christ here on earth. They also share the belief that the world will be improved, to varying degrees, by the spreading gospel. The differences between the two originate from the expected impact of the spreading gospel.

Post-millennialist have the expectation that the entire world will be Christianized and turned into a utopia, whereas amillennialist believe that during the millennium Satan is only hindered, so the battle between good and evil will continue until the second advent.[11]

Points of Strength:

There is strong scriptural evidence to suggest that people, who hear the gospel and accept it, change. When a person changes, their environment can be positively affected (cf. Matt. 5:13–16). Within that context, changed believers do their best to serve the Lord and improve the world where they live. It is the extent of that improvement that is in question.

Points of Weakness:

In this day and age, Christians are being met with increasing levels of hostility even though the gospel has been spread to the utmost regions of the world (John 15:18–19). There are even recent cases where believers lost their lives simply for loving the Lord. Consider the three children, who were kidnapped and beheaded, for attending a Christian school in an Indonesian country overrun by Islamic extremist (BBC News, October 2005). In several Middle Eastern countries, belief in Jesus as anything more than a prophet falls under the capital offense of apostasy. The world is clearly not getting better. That is why the post-millennialist expectation of a Christianized utopia is its greatest weakness (cf. Luke 21).

Pre-millennial Viewpoint

Basic Premises:

The last of the three viewpoints is pre-millennialism. Pre-millennialism is in–line with the futurist approach to Revelation. In other words, it looks to the future for the fulfillment of the millennial reign of Christ. The futurist approach stems largely from their interpretation of Revelation chapters 19 and 20. When taken literally, those verses show that the future return of Christ ushers in the establishment of his earthly kingdom and one–thousand–year reign.

At the end of those one thousand years, Satan will be loosed for a short time to deceive the nations again (Rev. 20:3–7). That deception leads to a final conflict between good and evil: the end result being the final destruction of evil in all of its forms. Therefore, in accordance with prophecy, there is no end to Christ's kingdom, just an upheaval during his reign (Dan. 7:14). His kingdom will continue into eternity (Rev. 20, 21).

Points of Strength:

The pre-millennialist viewpoint allows for a sound defense and presents a conceivable interpretation of the text. It is also somewhat in–line with other prophecies. Unlike the amillennialist approach, it does not adapt to "correct" perceived errors within the text.[12] God's words are infallible.[13] And, in comparison to the post-millennialist viewpoint, the deteriorating state of the world better fits the pre-millennialist chronology.

Points of Weakness:

The pre-millennialist approach, as with all approaches, has a common weakness, and that is interpretation. The reader must interpret apocalyptic imagery, at least to some degree.[14] In turn, they must understand that the imagery was first written in a different language.[15] Scholars who translated the texts must be trusted to have done their jobs well. With all of that in mind, there must be some understanding that the symbolism means something. It conveys clues about significant events. Therefore, the importance of the imagery relates to transitioning it to useful information.[16] The problem with that transition is deciding what the imagery means, and who decides what it means?

Many attempts at interpretation have already been made. Even unbelieving religious seers have written apocalyptic books and spoken ungodly prophecies. Their prophesies have left many unbelievers and believers alike frightened and confused. That is why pre-millennialist have to be careful not to accept every interpretation of end time prophecies.

The Lord warned that many false prophets would appear before his return (e.g. Matt. 24:11). Christians will know them by their works (Matt. 7:15–16). If their works only spread fear, then they are not from God, because God did not send his followers in a spirit of fear (2 Tim. 1:7). People who spread messages of fear are only sharing the hopelessness that is in them. If they knew God, and truly understood his plans for the end, their messages would not only reflect divine insight and completion, but also the hope he promised his people.

***

The previous section discussed major viewpoints on the millennial reign of Christ. The following section will discuss major viewpoints on the Apocalypse. Apocalyptic viewpoints have a lot in common with the millennialist schools of thought, so in some cases, you will read similar analysis and commentary.

Preterist Viewpoint

Basic Premises:

The origin of the preterist viewpoint can be traced back to the post-millennialist viewpoint.[17] Preterists take the position that the expectations of Revelation were largely fulfilled in the first century A.D., just before the fall of Jerusalem.[18] As such, that fulfillment is focused on the Roman invasion and destruction of the Jewish temple.

Points of Strength:

The preterist viewpoint is well presented and substantiated. To some degree, the first century Roman invasion does appear to fit certain fulfillment expectations. Historical documents further substantiate their viewpoint by painting vivid pictures of the events that unfolded during that time.[19]

Points of Weakness:

The problem with the preterist viewpoint is that it is dependent on the date Revelation was written. It had to be written prior to the Roman invasion for those events to be considered the fulfillment of apocalyptic events. Therein lies the problem. Many biblical scholars believe that Revelation was written long after the Roman invasion.[20] If those scholars are correct then the preterist viewpoint is wrong.[21] That is why preterists theologians have no choice but to vigorously dispute that claim.

Another problem is that preterism bares a striking resemblance to the false belief Paul refuted in 2 Thessalonians 2. Erroneous teachings and misunderstandings were leading some Christians to believe that the coming of the Lord occurred in the past. Paul refuted that belief by making it clear that the coming of the Lord would occur in the future (2:2). How far into the future is what preterists dispute.

Also notice the list of methods that were used to introduce that erroneous belief. One of those methods was forgery. Apparently, some Christians had received authoritative letters bearing the forged signatures of the apostles (cf. 2 Cor. 11:13, 2 Pet. 2:1). That is why Paul wrote that the letters appeared "as from us" (2:2). His point being that they were not from any of the real apostles. Understandably, 2 Thessalonians was written before the Roman invasion,[22] but the idea to place important apocalyptic events into the past was already being circulated in the Church.

There is also a great deal of debate concerning the way preterists interpret certain passages in Scripture. For example, in Matthew 16:28 the Lord told his disciples that some of them would not experience death until they saw him coming in his kingdom. Preterists take that to mean that the millennial reign was established while some of those disciples were still alive. Arguably, they have removed the distinction between the spiritual and visible kingdoms of God. They have also associated the millennial reign with the spiritual kingdom instead of the visible kingdom.

Jesus was a form of the spiritual kingdom. In fact, his glory will be the light of the future visible kingdom (Rev. 21:23–25). He chose to hide that light from an ungodly world, but did allow some of his disciples to see it. Just six days after making that promise, he took Peter, James, and John to a high mountaintop and showed them his glory–which is the glory of the coming kingdom (Matt. 17:1–9).

Another passage sometimes used to substantiate the preterist viewpoint is Luke 17:20–21. In those verses, the Lord tells the Pharisees that the kingdom of God cannot be seen. Taken at face value, that would appear to contradict futurist expectations of a visible kingdom on earth, but keep in mind that Jesus was responding to condescending Pharisees. His statements should be taken in that light.

Jesus is the prince of hosts because members of the Church host him in their bodies (cf. Dan. 8:11). Likewise, they are a part of his spiritual body (1 Cor. 3:16–17; 6:16–20; 12:13). That relationship cannot be seen or understood by unbelievers. For that reason, Jesus may have been telling the Pharisees that he was standing right in front of them, filled with all that is holy, yet they were so spiritually blind that they could not see him for what he was–the embodiment of the spiritual kingdom.[23] That kingdom is the unseen body of the Church that is "within you;" in other words, among you. Also notice the distinction between the unseen spiritual kingdom (verse 20) and later coming that everyone will see (verse 24).

In the parable of tares and wheat there was a span of time that occurred between the planting of the spiritual kingdom (seeds) and harvest of the wheat. During that time, good and evil were allowed to grow together. Only during the harvest will they be separated–one destroyed and the other taken into the barn. That barn is symbolic of the future visible kingdom, which is linked to the millennial reign. The growth of the seeds into wheat is symbolic of the growth the Church is experiencing now. That is why before it is gathered into the visible kingdom it must first be separated from internal and external evil (Matt. 13:30). That is how the perfect peace of the millennium will be established (cf. Isa. 2:4, 11:6).

The author C. Marvin Pate also raises an interesting contradiction to the preterist viewpoint. He asserts that the tribulations of John's lifetime fell under "the things which are [now]" category.[24] In other words, the persecution of the church in John's lifetime was clearly *a tribulation* but not *the Great Tribulation* that would fall under "the things which shall be hereafter" category, which points to the future.[25]

Idealist Viewpoint

Basic Premises:

The origin of the idealist viewpoint can be traced back to the Alexandrian church fathers.[26] Idealists view Revelation as an "ongoing conflict [between] good and evil, with no immediate historical connection to any social or political events."[27] In other words, Revelation is entirely symbolic with no relevance to actual events.

Points of Strength:

The idealist viewpoint has a timeless spiritual application for believers.[28] It is removed from the past or present, enabling its spiritual thematic to be applied by anyone in any period of time. The idealist approach can even be applied to the other three viewpoints. For example, preterists cannot deny that the first century persecution of the church was a struggle between good and evil. Dispensationalists may confirm yet another struggle in the future.

Points of Weakness:

The problem with the idealist viewpoint is that it fails to recognize the literal implications of other events in the bible that relate directly to Revelation and other apocalyptic texts. Those other events would have to be interpreted symbolically as well. Clearly that would pose a problem for proponents of this viewpoint.

With that in mind, recall how Jesus told the disciples he would send what God promised—that being the Holy Spirit (Luke 24:49). Prior to that, he told Mary not to touch him because he had not yet ascended to his Father in heaven (John 20:17). In Revelation 5:6, we find the literal fulfillment of those events as Jesus, symbolically shrouded as a lamb, ascended into the presence of his Father.

After offering himself for the sins of all humanity, he sent the "seven eyes" and "seven horns," which are the Holy Spirit, into the world. The events that occurred on the day of Pentecost validate that literal interpretation (Acts 2). That is why, even though Revelation is unique, it cannot be isolated from the rest of the Bible. It is also clear that the text has literal meanings veiled in symbolism.

Progressive Dispensationalist Viewpoint

Basic Premises:

Progressive dispensationalism originated in the 1980s when dispensational theologians rethought the classical viewpoint.[29] Progressive dispensationalists believe that Revelation depicts literal events.[30] Of those events, some have occurred already and some will occur in the future. Those two categories are referred to as "already" and "not yet."[31]

At its core is the belief that the resurrection and ascension of Christ resulted in the "inauguration of the kingdom."[32] Those events are considered the "already."[33] The next expected events are the return of Christ, and the establishment of his visible kingdom here on earth. Those events are considered the "not yet."[34]

Points of Strength:

Progressive dispensationalism not only supports the Revelation, but also other apocalyptic texts found in the synoptic gospels. Both historical and current events seem to be on track with the progressive viewpoint. Accordingly, there have been wars, rumors of wars, and famines, during this period of time between the first and second coming of Christ.

The war in Iraq, for example, was a prophetic event. It was a war based on the *rumors* that the Iraqi government had weapons of mass destruction (cf. Matt. 24:6, Mark 13:7). Now that fingers are being pointed, the origins of those rumors are still being pursued. Did the Central Intelligence Agency mislead the President? Did the President utilize propaganda to justify a war based on ulterior motives? Were the weapons there but too well hidden to be found? The list of questions goes on and on.

Whether or not you supported the war, you cannot deny that it was controversial and laden with rumors. Those rumors are just one example of many prophetic events that are unfolding during these last days. They are signs that we are heading towards the Great Tribulation (Matt. 24:8).

Points of Weakness:

Progressive dispensationalism is one of the stronger viewpoints because it fills in many blanks left open by preterism and idealism. Preterists cannot deny that the world is not shaping up to be a utopia, and idealists have to face the literal implications of Revelation's symbolism. On the downside, the progressive viewpoint shares the same inherent weakness as the premillennialist viewpoint, in that it leaves the "door" open to a multitude of prophecy buffs, who without inspiration from the Holy Spirit, capitalize on peoples' fears about the future.

Classical Dispensationalist Viewpoint

Basic Premises:

Classical dispensationalists, like progressive dispensationalists, use literal interpretations of Revelation. They share common beliefs because the progressive movement is an offshoot of the classical movement.[35] Even though that is the case, there are still notable differences. For example, progressive dispensationalists categorize the events in Revelation as either "already" or "not yet."[36] Classical dispensationalists, on the other hand, break the events down into specific periods of time.[37]

Points of Strength:

There are three factors that lend weight to the classical viewpoint. Those factors are: i) the literal interpretation of the text is conceivable; ii) there are strong literal tie-ins to other books in the Bible; iii) and, the periods of dispensation are reasonable methods for understanding both past and present events.

Points of Weakness:

The classical dispensationalist viewpoint shares similar points of weakness as those noted under pre-millennialism and progressive dispensationalism, the reason being that they all have in common the futurist approach. That has left the door open for a gauntlet of diverse interpretations.

NOTES

1. David MacLeod, "The Fourth 'Last Thing': The Millennial Kingdom of Christ (Rev. 20:4–6)," *Bibliotheca Sacra 157 (Jan., 2000): 44–67 (esp. 50–51).*

2. Ibid., 49.

3. Ibid., 49.

4. Ibid., 49. The word "amillennial" can be broken down into "a" which means "no" and "millennial" from the two Latin words "mille" and "ennium." Together, they mean "no millennium." http://www.merriam-webster.com/dictionary/millennium on the Latin for "millennium".

5. Sam Hamstra Jr., "An Idealist View of Revelation" in *Four Views on the Book of Revelation,* eds. Stanley Gundry and C. Marvin Pate (Grand Rapids: Zondervan, 1998), 120–121. Luke 10:18 is an interesting verse to compare to Revelation 20:2, because it only mentions that Satan fell, but does not mention his binding.

6. Ibid., 120–121.

7. Ibid., 120–121.

8. Satan was able to offer Jesus Christ the kingdoms of this world because he became the god of this world. It is also why the Lord will physically take them back in the future (cf. Ephesians 2:2, Revelation 11:15).

9. MacLeod, *"The Fourth 'Last Thing': The Millennial Kingdom of Christ (Rev. 20:4–6),"* (Jan. 2000), 50–51.

10. Ibid., 51.

11. Ibid., 51.

12. Richard L. Mayhue, "Jesus: A Preterist or Futurist?" in *The Master's Seminary Journal* 14:1 (Spring, 2003): 9–22

(esp. 11–13). Though it addresses R.C. Sproul's book, which involves a preterist approach to the Revelation, the implications to amillennialism are clear.

13. God's words are infallible but Christians should be mindful that the same infiltrators that blended in with the Church have introduced doctrines and publications that they claim are God's word.

14. Gordon D. Fee and Douglas Stuart, *How to Read the Bible for all its Worth.* (Grand Rapids: Zondervan, 2003). 18–19.

15. Ibid., 18–19.

16. Vern Poythress, "Genre and Hermeneutics in Rev. 20:1-6," *Journal of the Evangelical Theological Society* 36 (March 1993). 41-54. (esp. 43).

17. See the "The Preterist Interpretation" in *Four Views on the Book of Revelation,* by Kenneth L. Gentry Jr., Sam Hamstra Jr., C. Marvin Pate and Robert L. Thomas, eds. Stanley N. Gundry and C. Marvin Pate (Grand Rapids: Zondervan, 1998), 20.

18. Kenneth L. Gentry, "A Preterist View of Revelation" in *Four Views on the Book of Revelation,* eds. Stanley Gundry and C. Marvin Pate (Grand Rapids: Zondervan, 1998), 37. See also page 17 in the introduction section.

19. See footnotes and commentary on the writings of Flavius Josephus, in the *Four Views of the Revelation,* 54–55.

20. Michael A. Harbin, *The Promise and the Blessing: A Historical Survey of the Old and New Testaments.* (Grand Rapids: Zondervan, 2005). 579.

21. Craig S. Keener, *The NIV Application Commentary: Revelation.* (Grand Rapids: Zondervan, 2000). 35–39.

22. Bible: TNIV. *Today's New International Version: Study Bible.* (Grand Rapids: Zondervan, 2006). 2021. Cf. 2 Tim. 2:18.

23. It is of note that John wrote that he was a companion in the kingdom (spiritual body) and patience of Christ (Rev.

1:9). Later, he described the physical kingdom the Lord will establish as the physical counterpart for that spiritual body of the Church (Rev. 11:15). Therefore, he indirectly made a distinction between the two.

24. C. Marvin Pate, "A Progressive Dispensationalist View of Revelation" in *Four Views on the Book of Revelation*, eds. Stanley Gundry and C. Marvin Pate (Grand Rapids: Zondervan, 1998), 137.

25. Ibid., 137.

26. See introduction, *Four Views on the Book of Revelation* for more information on the Alexandrian church fathers, 24.

27. Taken from *Four Views on the Book of Revelation* by Kenneth L. Gentry Jr., Sam Hamstra Jr., C. Marvin Pate and Robert L. Thomas, eds. Stanley N. Gundry and C. Marvin Pate. Copyright© 1998 by C. Marvin Pate, Kenneth L. Gentry Jr., Sam Hamstra, Robert L. Thomas. Used by permission of Zondervan. www.zondervan.com. See page 23.

28. Sam Hamstra Jr., "An Idealist View of Revelation" in *Four Views on the Book of Revelation,* eds. Stanley Gundry and C. Marvin Pate (Grand Rapids: Zondervan, 1998), 128–129.

29. See "Progressive Dispensationalism" in *Four Views on the Book of Revelation,* by Kenneth L. Gentry Jr., Sam Hamstra Jr., C. Marvin Pate and Robert L. Thomas, eds. Stanley N. Gundry and C. Marvin Pate (Grand Rapids: Zondervan, 1998), 31.

30. Ibid., 29.

31. Ibid., 31.

32. Taken from *Four Views on the Book of Revelation* by Kenneth L. Gentry Jr., Sam Hamstra Jr., C. Marvin Pate and Robert L. Thomas, eds. Stanley N. Gundry and C. Marvin Pate. Copyright© 1998 by C. Marvin Pate, Kenneth L. Gentry Jr., Sam Hamstra, Robert L. Thomas. Used by permission of Zondervan. www.zondervan.com. See page 31.

33. See "Progressive Dispensationalism" in *Four Views on the Book of Revelation,* by Kenneth L. Gentry Jr., Sam Hamstra Jr., C. Marvin Pate and Robert L. Thomas, eds. Stanley N. Gundry and C. Marvin Pate. (Grand Rapids: Zondervan, 1998), 31.

34. Ibid., 31.

35. Ibid., 30–33

36. Ibid., 31.

37. Ibid., 28–29.

And why it will be
so severe!!!

2. MISSED WARNINGS

rguably, the problem inherit with those major viewpoints is that they overlook the purpose of the Great Tribulation. They also miss many of the warnings contained in end time prophecies. Contrary to popular beliefs, those warnings are the main reasons the apocalyptic texts were written. That is why, even the stronger viewpoints have not adequately prepared Christians for the events that will precede the return of Christ. Outside of the gospel of salvation, those warnings are next in the line of importance.

When asked about his return, the Lord replied with a wealth of information, but he also said something that should raise an eyebrow. He said, "I have told you before" (Matt. 24:25). Even though that statement directly relates to that particular passage, you have to keep in mind that the Word of God was providing apocalyptic information long before his incarnation as the man Jesus Christ (cf. John 1:1–14). That is why that same statement indirectly sets the stage for all end time prophecies, even those found in the Old Testament.

God passed that information down through the ages, because there would come a time when he would not communicate so directly with his Church (John 14:30). His intention was to have it forwarded to the generation of faithful servants who would witness those events (cf. Dan. 12:4, Rev. 22:10). He wants them to be prepared. He also wants them to understand why the tribulation has to be severe.

Evil servants are deeply embedded in the Church and will not leave without cause. That is why God must give them cause by shaking the foundations of this world the same way he shook the boat carrying the apostles (cf. Isa. 13:8–13, Matt. 24:13, Mark 13:13).[1] That storm was under

Anti Christ
+ false prophets   false messiahs

17

his control, and the end time tribulation will be under his control (cf. Mark 4:39, Matt. 24:29–31). The distractions of the storm exposed the depth of the apostles' faith. Likewise, the end time tribulation will expose the true faith of each and every Christian in his Church. Those who are not sincere will be led away at that time.

The Trap

Evil servants appeared at the same time Christianity started to spread. They expanded their reach by keeping pace with the growing Church. That is why in Matthew 13:26, the tares sprung up with the wheat. The generations that modeled the ways of those evil servants are still here among the "wheat," working evil deeds in God's name.

Evil servants called on the name of the Lord and were saved, but turned on their fellow servants (2 Pet. 2:1–22). That is why there was a concern about harvesting them together. God will address that concern with a trap designed to lure evil servants away (Matt. 13:26–30). The details about his trap are contained in many apocalyptic texts. Those details were intended to heighten the awareness of discerning Christians.

Awareness is key because anyone caught unaware will be susceptible to the traps deception (Matt. 24:24, Mark 13:22). In fact, that is why evil servants will be deceived. They are already blinded by the same false expectations they used to deceive their fellow servants (cf. 2 Cor. 11:15, 2 Thess. 2:11–12). To add to their delusion, for a short time God will allow it to appear as if the things they promised were true. Remember that the condemned mentioned prophecy as one of their gifts. They would not mention that gift unless at some point in time their prophecies started to come true. That validation of power will cause many of them to become complacent. Why? Because they will think they are on the right path to righteousness (cf. Matt. 24:50). In that state of complacency, they will be seduced into accepting deceptive doctrines designed to lure them toward God's trap.

That is why the Apocalypse and other related passages are so important. They contain God's plans for the end. The fact that some of the information is veiled only relates to timing. It had not yet reached its intended audience. When it did, God would gift some of his servants with discernment and interpretation to reveal its contents.

Gifts of Ministries

Having said that, it is important to understand that not every Christian was or will be inspired by the Holy Spirit to reveal end time prophecies. Some were inspired to know and teach the Old Testament; others the New. There are designated roles in the Church (cf. 1 Cor. 12:28–31). Those who are gifted to teach one aspect of Scripture, with ease, may find other parts difficult. That has nothing to do with faith, only job description.

The problem arises when Church leaders feel pressured to teach outside of their designated ministries. If you look at the way the Bible was compiled over the centuries, with contributions made by God's servants—some big, some small—you will understand that not knowing one part of Scripture does not diminish, in any way, a valid contribution pertaining to another. Every valid contribution is meant to edify the Church. When those contributions are pieced together with the whole, sometimes over centuries, God's massive plans are revealed.

Some Church leaders are teaching on things that were not inspired by the Holy Spirit. They are taking grievous liberties with their positions. That is one of the reasons why the Lord warned, "many shall come in my name, saying, I am Christ; and shall deceive many" (Matt. 24:5). Who comes in the name of Jesus Christ with the message that he is the Messiah? Christians! Notice the future tense "shall come."

The founder of the Christian Church warned that something about later Christian teachings that relate to his return would contribute to the deception of many people. The fact that many will be deceived indicates that these teachings are very well known.

Unfortunately, some of the people spreading deception are deceived themselves. They unknowingly adopted false teachings because they were viewed as authoritative and trustworthy. They, in turn, presented those false teachings to many other people. That is why the deception is so widespread. Those teachings are prophetic, and actually act as time markers for the other events that will unfold.

The Test Begins

Those other events will begin after a marked increase in the frequency, scale, and intensity of natural disasters, wars, and famines (Luke 21). That is when fear and hopelessness will enter the minds of many people (Luke

21:26). Those things are only a part of the delusion God will send. They create the "storm" that sets the stage for his test.

It is during that "storm" that God will loose a false messiah on the earth (cf. 2 Thess. 2:8–12). Evil servants will wrongly identify with him and receive him with a great amount of joy (John 14:30, Matt. 24:21–27). They will be so relieved at the sight of their messiah that they will spread the good news about his return (cf. 2 Cor. 11:14–15). They will not realize that the true Messiah will still be in heaven, observing the hypocrisy of their faith (Matt. 24:21–30).

The Lord will watch as the false Christ teaches them to turn away from their core beliefs (2 Thess. 2:3). He will seduce them into following a deceptive religious system that centers on a dangerous device that will lead to their damnation. That is why not all people who cry out "Lord, Lord, shall enter into the kingdom of heaven" (Matt. 7:21). Those evil servants will be severed from the blood covenant. As you will see in a later chapter, they will be so deceived that even their cry is an insult to the true Jesus Christ.

Christian vs. Christian

The Lord's warning was very clear, and that was to stay away from the false messiah, his ministers of light, and the deceived people who follow them (cf. Matt. 24:10, 2 Cor. 11:15, 1 Tim. 4:1). He does not want faithful Christians caught up in their delusion. That may be easier said than done, because in some cases those people will be friends and family. Many of those relationships will be torn apart (Matt. 10:21, 10:35–37, Mark 13:12, Luke 21:16–17).

That spiritual rift, between members of the Church, is the result of a "collision" between certain viewpoints and the truth about the apocalypse. That rift will cause two lines of Christians to form with conflicting messages. Those lines are already developing, but will become more defined as time progresses. In the end, they will actually oppose each other, with one side appearing to gain the upper hand (cf. Matt. 24:48–51).

That upper hand coincides with the false messiah granting his people power and authority. As they misused their positions in the Church, they will misuse their positions as the false righteous and turn on those faithful servants who refuse to accept their Christ (cf. Matt. 10:17–22). That is when they will be revealed for who they are-children of the wicked one (Matt. 13:38).

The Last Generation

The Lord's reference to a generation that would witness the events of the apocalypse points to the last generation of the Church (Matt. 24:34). In other words, all of those turbulent events would occur within the lifetime of that generation. Some interpret that verse to mean the audience he was talking to that day, but it has to be read in the context of future events. The remnant of that future generation would see his plans unfold. Therefore, the end time tribulation begins and ends during a predetermined span of time (Dan. 12:11). It is during that time that faithful Christians will have to demonstrate that they are ready for the greater things the Lord put aside for them.[2]

***

The question Christians should ask is why do they need to understand the end time tribulation if they will not be here to go through it? Isn't that what many of them are being taught? Aren't they going to be caught up, in the twinkling of an eye, before it begins (1 Cor. 15:51–52)? Won't they be spared from its horrors, or is there something wrong with that viewpoint (cf. 2 Tim. 3:16)? To find the answers to those questions, there must first be an understanding of how apocalyptic information was passed down through the ages.

NOTES

1. Matt. 24:22 reveals that the turmoil of that time will be so intense that if God did not limit its timeframe no one would be alive when he returned.

2. Cf. Matt. 6:19.

3. THE CRITIQUE AND THE PACKAGE

I magine for a moment a meeting of world leaders. An editor wants accurate accounts of the meeting to publish an article for his readers. In order to do that, he sends two of his best reporters to cover the story. One reporter covers the meeting from outside the building. The other reporter covers it from inside. The next day, the reporter stationed outside was able to provide a written account of who showed up and what time they arrived. The reporter stationed inside provided a written account of what was discussed. The reporters' observations were different but related to the same meeting. The editor was able to compile their information to put together a fairly detailed article for his readers.

God passed apocalyptic information to his Church in a similar way. He gave some of his servants multiple accounts of the same end time events, through visions, dreams, or teachings that conveyed to this later time in the form of the written or spoken word. It is now a matter of piecing the many accounts together for a better understanding of what will take place in the future.

Consider how many separate accounts Daniel presented in that one book (Dan. 7:7–13, 8:9–25, 11, 12). Each of those accounts bares an apocalyptic punctuation mark: the second advent of Christ[1]. Also notice how Daniel 9:27 and 11:31 mentions the same desecration of the temple, the same abolishment of the daily sacrifice, and the same setting up of an abominable image. That is because they are different accounts of the same events.

For comparison, notice the difference between two accounts of the second advent. In one account Jesus is called Faithful and True (Rev. 19:11). In another account he is called the Son of Man (Dan. 7:13). Even though the Lord's name is different in each account, both describe his return. Other servants of God shared similar enlightenment as they too were given different accounts of the apocalypse (e.g. Zech. 14:9–16, 2 Thess. 2:8–12).

In addition to understanding multiple perspectives, it is important to know that some apocalyptic texts contain imagery that means something. Imagery was not selected at random without reason; rather, the imagery was picked to convey specific information to faithful Christians.

That is how God was able to convey such vast amounts of information through the ages. He compartmentalized it, in some cases veiled it, and disseminated it to his servants to be pieced together at a later time in history. That is why many accounts appear strewn throughout Scripture. Revelation, on the other hand, groups many accounts into one book. It contains one of the largest compilations of apocalyptic perspectives in the Bible. For that reason, it is important to understand its framework before trying to understand its contents.

The Critique

Revelation begins with seven letters "addressed" to seven churches that existed during John's lifetime (cf. Acts 16:5). The letters served as critiques intended to point out the strengths and weaknesses of each church. The intended recipients of those letters were the members of those churches. That was "the things which are [now]" portion of the text (Rev. 1:19).

A part of that critique entailed a detailed description of how each church would progress through time. The Lord saw them from beginning to end and gave an assessment of not only their current state (at that time) but also their end state (at a later time). He was able to provide that information because time is not a factor for God.

***

The Package

Along with that critique came a special "package" of information. That information was to be guarded and passed down throughout the ages until it reached its intended audience. That was "the things which shall be hereafter" portion of the text (Rev. 1:19). Therefore, Revelation contains both a critique for the churches of John's time and a special package of information to be forwarded to the last generation of the faithful Church. Within that package are many individual accounts of events that will bring about the end of this age. When pieced together, they reveal a fairly detailed picture of God's plans.

NOTES

1. The second advent is a common event found in those
   particular verses, however, it is not found in every account of
   the apocalypse.

4. UNVEILING THE UNHOLY TRINITY

Revelation 19:20 identifies two important characters that rise and fall during the tribulation. It states, "and the beast was taken, and with him the false prophet that wrought miracles before him… both were cast alive into a lake of fire burning with brimstone." From that passage we know that at the end of the tribulation, the Lord will judge and punish the beast and false prophet.

A third character is identified in the very next chapter, but his punishment will not take place until after the millennial reign is fulfilled (Rev. 20:7–10). Revelation 20:10 states, "and the devil that deceived them was [also] cast into the lake of fire and brimstone, where the beast and the false prophet are." Therefore, the devil is the third part of the unholy trinity.

To clarify, the beast and false prophet will be cast into the lake of fire immediately after the Great Tribulation. The devil, however, will only be bound at that time because he has another purpose to fulfill at the end of the millennial reign. That purpose is to deceive (test) the nations again (Rev. 20:7–8). When that purpose is fulfilled he will join the beast and false prophet in the lake of fire.

Members of that unholy trinity appear in many accounts of the apocalypse. Each account contains compartmentalized information that relates directly or indirectly to each character. It is now a matter of gathering the information from each account and compiling it with the whole.

Death and Hell

In Revelation chapter 6, the Lord opens a seal that unleashes a powerful conqueror on the earth. Incidentally, this account is one of the longest in Revelation, beginning in chapter 4 and ending in chapter 11. The imagery used in this perspective is that of four horses with distinct coloring. Read carefully and notice that the horses change but the rider remains the same. At first his identity is hidden, as it will be hidden from the world.

Just to be clear, there is one rider using four different horses in quick succession. The horses denote speed and public opinion. His rise to power will be quick, as the world views him by the color of his horses. He will come in riding a white horse, so he will be perceived as a bringer of peace. Public opinion will change as his horses change. When he transitions to the last horse, his name is revealed—Death. Death is the horseman; the only horseman. Also notice that the name "Death" is not mentioned in Revelation 20:10 because the name itself is another example of the imagery used to shroud his identity.

The naming of that sole horseman as Death should sufficiently negate any belief that the white horse rider represents the Holy Spirit loosed into the world. That event already occurred in Revelation 5:6. It should also negate the all too common misconception that there are four separate riders. There is only one, and he is evil. His name is not revealed until the end because people will not know who he is at first.

Closer examination of that same imagery shows that each subsequent horse is the result of the actions of the previous horse. His peace leads to war. His war leads to famine. His famine leads to death—hence the name, so even his name has meaning. The imagery here gives us insight into the actions of the beast, the results of those actions, and the method he will use to establish his kingdom.

In a different perspective of Death's rise to power, Daniel addressed the issue of the white horse. He wrote, "by peace [Death] shall destroy many" (Dan. 8:25). With that verse, Daniel confirmed John's account. Peace is the first "tool" Death will use to establish his kingdom. There is also another important clue in this account.

Look closely at the text and notice that Death is followed by someone else—Hell. As you will see, Hell is the false prophet, who (in almost every account) follows the appearance of the beast. Also note that as with the horses, the names "Death" and "Hell" show successive events. Those who follow (submit to or worship) this duo will die a horrible *death*, ending up in eternal *hell* caused by the lake of fire.[1]

So, two of the three characters in Revelation 20:10 have been identified in this vision. The third character is not mentioned, but his actions are implied. Daniel 8:24, notes that "his [Death's] power shall be mighty, but not by his own power." In Revelation chapter 6, you will notice words like "given" and "granted," meaning his power was given to him. In Revelation 13:3, a different account, we find that the source of that power is the Devil (cf. Dan. 8:24).

The Devil's Authority

The Devil offered Jesus Christ the kingdoms of this world because they were his to give (Matt. 4:8–9). That demonic authority stems from Adam's fall. Adam was a king, in a sense, so by disobeying God and following a path of sin, he unknowingly submitted his authority to the Devil. That is also why the Devil wanted Jesus to worship him (verse 9).

If one king bows to or serves another, there is a submission of authority. One king gains power over the other. That is how the Devil became the god of this world and a curse (2 Cor. 4:4, Eph. 2:2). That is also why Jesus will physically claim the kingdoms of this world when he returns (John 12:31, Rev. 11:15).

Beasts from the Earth and Sea

To find another perspective on the rise of the beast and false prophet, we go to Revelation chapter 13. This account actually begins in chapter 12, but the evil trinity is not observed together until chapter 13. Chapter 12 gives some reasons for the Devil's anger toward mankind, in particular, Israel. It describes his fall and war with God. It also touches on the institution of the authority of Christ. Therefore, some accounts go far beyond the tribulation into the before and after. There are also some that go into the heavenly realms (Rev. 4, 5).

Revelation chapter 13 does not use the names Death and Hell. Here, the imagery is that of beasts rising from the earth and sea. The first beast has seven heads and ten horns. The imagery of heads and horns gives us the set up of Death's government. Seven heads represent his "congress." They will be his minds or thinkers (e.g. heads of authority or law makers). Horns represent authorities with domain, so the ten horns represent subordinate kings and their kingdoms. This is clearly describing a future event because the ten horns have received no power yet and will not until the appearance of the beast (Rev. 17:12).

Note in this perspective how the focus shifts from how Death rises (the four horses) to the hierarchy and structure of his kingdom (seven heads and ten horns). This account also delves deeper into the relationship between the unholy trinity.

To recap, the first beast is observed rising from the sea (Rev. 13:1–2). The second beast then follows the same way Hell followed Death in the previous account. The Devil is also found in Revelation 12 and 13:2–4. So, all three characters from Revelation 20:10 are present in this perspective as well.

Four Beasts

Daniel chapter 7 contains yet another perspective on the rise of the beast and false prophet. In this vision, Daniel observes four beasts that rise from the sea. There has been a great deal of debate on which kingdoms those four beasts represent. In some cases, the argument was made that they represent ancient kingdoms. In other cases, the argument is that they represent the kingdoms of our present world. The angel that was sent to interpret the vision placed the most emphasis on the fourth and final kingdom, so the focus of this discussion will be the same.

Notice that the fourth kingdom precedes the appearance of a little horn (Dan. 7:7–8, 7:23–25). Also notice that the little horn commits the same offenses against God and his people as the second beast found in Revelation chapter 13. This is no coincidence. That fourth beast is yet another example of how imagery was used to shroud Death and his kingdom. Out of that kingdom, once again following Death, comes Hell, the little horn.

That fourth kingdom has not yet appeared because, as you will see, there has been no kingdom on earth that fits the criteria of Death's theocracy. There is also the matter of the Lord Jesus Christ warring with that fourth kingdom in Revelation chapter 19. The text is clear in that during the aftermath of that war, the beast and false prophet are taken *alive*, so that cannot point to a past event (Rev. 19:20).

The Goat and Ram

Daniel's next vision also provides another interesting perspective on the rise of the fourth kingdom, but the imagery this time is that of a warring goat battling a ram (Dan. 8). When the angel Gabriel interpreted the symbolism, he revealed that the goat and ram are kingdoms that rise on the earth during the last days of man (verse 17–19). Subsequently, the goat wins the battle.

The four horns that rise out of the first larger horn are the four kingdoms, symbolized as beasts, in the previous account (Dan. 7). That previous vision also showed the sequence in which those four kingdoms (horns) would rise. In this vision, however, those four kingdoms are, for lack of better words, glossed over to place emphasis on the actions of the little horn (Dan. 8:9).

"Improving" Scripture

Understanding that perspectives of end time events were discretely and indiscreetly strewn throughout Scripture should demonstrate the need to maintain the exactness of God's words. That means that even if a scholar is biased towards one viewpoint, he or she must still ensure that they are not changing or "improving" verses for purposes of readability. There are now many versions of Scripture on the market that have completely removed or altered apocalyptic accounts because of a failure to look beyond the filters put in place by particular viewpoints.

One of the more notable examples is found in Isaiah 14:12 where the name "Lucifer" is sometimes changed or removed. That account was not only a chastisement of the King of Babylon; it was also an apocalyptic overlay. A Christian reader, not familiar with the King James Version, would understand that passage completely differently than God intended.[2]

Another controversial account is found in Ezekiel 28. In that chapter the Lord spoke a prophecy against the king of Tyrus. The prophecy is the more obvious purpose of the text, but one can reason that the king of Tyrus was never an anointed cherub, who walked in the garden of God. Simply disregarding those discrepancies, or trying to explain them away as unique to the language of that time, removes the insight about the Devil that God wanted to convey to his Church. That is why Christians should be mindful not to accept every version of Scripture as the infallible word of God. Many have been altered in ways that will drastically change their understanding of his words.

NOTES

1. In this instance, hell means torment not the bottomless pit that is deep inside the earth (cf. 2 Pet. 2:4, Jude 1:6). The bottomless pit is often described as having gates that are locked (Matt. 16:18). There is no water and the fire produces a strange dark light (Luke 16:23–24, Job 10:21–22, Rev. 9:1–2). In regards to Luke 16:23–24, Lazarus was able to see the bottomless pit because he was directly across from it in a temporary paradise. The reason for that paradise will be in the subject matter of a later chapter.

2. The point of mentioning the King James Version here was only to raise awareness of changes to apocalyptic texts. The author is in no way trying to discourage the use of other credible versions of the Bible. In fact, he recommends using multiple versions, with scholarly commentary, to enhance the readers understanding of Scripture.

5. DANIEL 9:25–27 DISCUSSED

Another step in exploring the Apocalypse is to discuss one of the more controversial passages in Scripture, Daniel 9:25–27. Even though it is short, it contains important apocalyptic information. Along with that information is mention of a person referred to only as "he." The angel who conveyed the information revealed that "he" would be so influential that he will change established religious practices and set up a covenant during a turbulent time (verse 27). Those actions demonstrate the high level of his authority.

The problem is that even though the angel provided detailed information about his actions, he did not provide much information about his identity. For that reason, scholarly debate has resulted in several extremes. On one side "he" is believed to be Christ; on another side, "he" is believed to be the antichrist.[1] Yet another group believes "he" was Titus, the first century conquering prince who destroyed the temple. This chapter will discuss those viewpoints.

"He" is Christ

Basic Premises:

The possibility that "he" is Christ is based on the notion that his actions fulfill messianic prophecy. Arguably, his most significant action is the confirmation of a covenant. That covenant, when viewed in a positive light, gives weight to the belief that "he" is Christ.[2] In regards to taking away the daily sacrifice, Edward J. Young believed that it was the result of the ultimate sacrifice made by Jesus.[3] With positive parallels like those in mind, one can make a strong case that "he" is Christ.

Points of Strength:

Since Daniel's prayer was rooted in several of Jeremiah's prophecies, one can assume that the angels answer was also rooted the same way.[4] One prophecy, in particular, ends with the promise of a better covenant following Israel's seventy years of turmoil (Jer. 31:31–34). Therefore, the angel may have been telling Daniel that "he" was the prophetic fulfillment and mediator of that better covenant found in Jeremiah's prophecy.[5]

Another significant point to consider is the content of Daniel's prayer in relation to the angel's purpose. Daniel was asking about his people's redemption, which he challenged God to hear (9:19). He prayed for God to turn his anger away from them and shine on the sanctuary (9:16–17). With that in mind, why would the angel respond to Daniel with news that ended on a bad note? Therefore, the reference to "he" could be related to Christ, who is the one who would bring about that restoration.

Points of Weakness:

The inherit weakness with identifying "he" as Christ is that all of his actions would have to viewed in light of other Scripture. Jesus is God; therefore, his approach to covenants can be assessed throughout the Bible.[6] Scripture reveals that God never broke a covenant. It was the people who failed. If "he" is Christ, then why would he suddenly step out of character and break a covenant? Even punishments were laid out in the laws of God's covenants.[7] In verse 27; the abominable actions committed in the middle of the covenant, by the same person who confirmed it, leads one to believe that it was broken (cf. Dan. 7:25). That is a significant problem for those who hold to the belief that "he" is Christ.

"He" is the False Prophet

Basic Premises:

The negative actions that immediately follow the "he" of Daniel 9:27 leads one to believe that he is at odds with God. Jesus was not, and never has been, at odds with his father. They are one. The thought of the Lord setting up something in the temple that the angel would call an abomination is unconscionable (cf. Dan. 11:32). Since he is affecting religious worship in an abominable way, it is clear that he is an embodiment of evil. An abomination will only separate people from God. Therefore, in accordance with the criteria listed for the makings of a false prophet, "he" best fits that description (Deut. 13:1–5).[8]

Points of Strength:

The strongest point of this belief is that it is substantiated by other apocalyptic texts. Daniel did not have just one vision of end time events; he had many (cf. Dan. 7:7–13, 8:9–25, 11–12). Consider Daniel 11:31 where he mentions the same desecration of the temple, the same abolishment of daily sacrifice, and the same setting up of an abominable image noted in 9:27. Those accounts run parallel to each other. The difference between the two is that 11:31 contains much more information about who "he" is. Based on that additional information, one can surmise that the "he" mentioned in Daniel 9:27 is also the little horn mentioned in Daniel 7:8–11. Daniel also observes him two other times taking away the daily sacrifice (8:11, 11:31). The negative actions of this person are very clear in chapter 8, where it is noted that he will destroy the holy people and rise against the Prince of princes (verse 25).

Points of Weakness:

The weakness of this viewpoint stems from the very prayer that initiated the angel's response. Daniel wanted an immediate answer in regard to Israel's punishment and restoration (9:19). The angel even sounded hurried by revealing to Daniel that the command went out at the very beginning of Daniel's supplications. In other words, his prayer was not even over before God sent him. With that in mind, one has to consider why his answer would be fulfilled thousands of years in the future.

"He" is Titus

Basic Premises:

The belief that "he" is Titus stems mostly from the preterist school of thought. They take the position that the expectations of Revelation were fulfilled when Titus invaded and destroyed the holy temple. That is why many of them view Titus as the prophetic embodiment of "he."

Points of Strength:

As stated before, preterism is well presented and substantiated. To some degree, the first century invasion and destruction of the temple does appear to fit certain fulfillment expectations of Daniel 9:27.

Points of Weakness:

The problem with this viewpoint stems from the actions of Titus. He did fulfill a portion of prophecy dealing directly with the destruction of the temple (9:26). However, he did not fulfill the remainder of the prophecy. In verse 27, "he" is committing abominable actions in the temple (cf. Dan. 11:31, 12:11).[10] How is the temple once again there? The temple was destroyed and remains in ruins to this day. Only the Western Wall still stands. Therefore, this must point to a future event that remains to be fulfilled. Interestingly enough, an organization in Israel is prepared to rebuild the future temple at a moment's notice.[11]

NOTES

1. Stephen R. Miller, *The New American Commentary: Daniel*, Vol. 18. (Nashville: B&H, 1994), 270–271.

2. Ibid., 270.

3. Edward J. Young, *The Prophecy of Daniel* (Grand Rapids: Eerdmans, 1949), 208, mentioned in Stephen R. Miller, *The New American Commentary: Daniel*, Vol. 18. (Nashville: B&H, 1994), 270.

4. Tremper Longman III, *The NIV Application Commentary: Daniel*. Grand Rapids, Michigan, 1999. 236–237.

5. Ibid., 234–237. Cf. Jer. 31:31–34, 1 Tim. 2:5, and Heb. 8:6–12.

6. Gordon D. Fee and Douglas Stuart, *How to Read the Bible for all its Worth*. Grand Rapids: Zondervan, 2003. 164-168.

7. Ibid., 164-168.

8. Cf. Revelation 13.

9. Kenneth L. Gentry, "A Preterist View of Revelation" in *Four Views on the Book of Revelation*, eds. Stanley N. Gundry and C. Marvin Pate (Grand Rapids: Zondervan, 1998), 37. See also page 17 in the introduction for a brief synopsis of that basis.

10. Consulting other versions of Scripture, preferably with scholarly commentary, is recommended for comparison and better understanding of that verse.

11. See the official Temple Institute website for more: http://www.templeinstitute.org/main.htm

6. THE HASTY ADVENT

Daniel 7:24 mentions that during the rise of the false prophet he will defeat three warring kings. Those kings will pose an immediate danger to Jerusalem. Because of that threat, many Christians will consider those kings evil. The opposite of evil is good, so Hell's war campaign against them will appear, to some, as good.[1] Christians, who do not heed apocalyptic warnings, will relate his war to the war mentioned in Revelation 19. In doing so, they will mistake the false prophet's appearance for the second advent of Christ (2 Cor. 11:14). Why? Because his appearance and actions will be in–line with their expectations for a hasty intervention by the messiah.

Those expectations stem from their understandings of certain passages in Scripture. For example, Luke 21:19–27 mentions that at some point in the future, enemies will pose an imminent danger to Jerusalem. The context of those verses does create a sense of urgency. The problem is that some teachings focus only on that urgency and create a careless bridge directly to the last event–the second advent of Christ (verse 20). That bridge closes the gap between the two events, so the sense of urgency is understood incorrectly.

Notice how the Lord used the word "patience" right before providing information about the subsequent events that faithful Christians "shall see" (verse 19). It is as if he wanted them to know that they should remain patient while the rest of the world panicked.[2] In other words, they would see those events but not participate in the confusion that followed. Also notice how patience is related to the protection of the soul (verse 19). The Lord's point being that patience will be the key to enduring those events. Patience removes them from the panic that the world will give in to.

39

In regards to the sense of urgency; that relates directly to "the desolation thereof [that] is nigh"(verse 20). The Lord was warning Christians that when enemies surround Jerusalem, something that caused desolation would be physically present on the earth.[3] In our discussions about Daniel 9:25–27, Hell and his religious system were identified as abominations. While referring to those abominations, the Lord said that they would cause desolation (cf. Matt. 24:15, Mark 13:14). Therefore, his reference to the end time desolation is a warning about the false prophet's fully operational religious system. That prophetic time marker is when Christians will see a great deal of panic and confusion caused by the increasing intensity of the tribulation. During that time, the Lord does not want faithful Christians to become impatient like the "tares" he will root out.

Faith that Fell on Stony Places

In the parable of the evil servant, it was a delay in the lord's coming that brought about drastic changes in that servant's behavior (Matt. 24:48). Likewise, during the end time tribulation, the behavior of many unfaithful Christians will drastically change because of the Lord's "delay." To them, he will have failed by not taking them away before the tribulation. That "delay" will be more than enough to cause many of them to abandon their faith (cf. 2 Pet. 3:3–4, 3:9–15).

Other unfaithful Christians, who are more deeply embedded in the Church, will not go so easily. They will, however, become increasingly impatient as their wait continues. During their impatience, God will expose them to increasing levels of "heat" (Matt. 13:5–6; 24:13). It is during that time that they will demonstrate the hypocrisy of their faith by doubting the accomplishments and coming of the Lord. Their doubt will later deteriorate into offense (Matt. 13:20–21).

To add to their predicament, their false prophets and ministers of light will adapt their teachings to better fit the timeline of Hell's appearance. That is why when many of them see or hear about his great victory against the enemies of Jerusalem, they will hastily accept him as Christ (cf. 2 Cor. 11:14, Rev. 13:14). In doing so, they will unknowingly accept Hell's false light as hope and look away from the true Light of the world (John 1:7).

It is ironic but the false prophet's offer of hope, during the end time tribulation, is the same false hope many evil servants offered people who also suffered tribulations. It is God's fitting punishment that they should be deceived in the same way. Likewise, the things they hear will be deceiving.

Scripture warns that the false prophet will speak ungodly sentences and teach deceptive doctrines (Dan. 8:23, 1 Tim. 4:1). That is why he looks like a lamb but speaks like a dragon (Rev. 13:11). Everything about his appearance is just a ruse to get unfaithful Christians to listen to his lies.

To further legitimize his appearance, Hell will be allowed to wield gifts that resemble those granted by the Holy Spirit. Unfaithful Christians will not realize that they stem from the Devil and amount to nothing more than sorcery (cf. Acts 8:9, Rev. 9:21, 13:14, 16:14, 19:20). That is the other irony of God's trap. The same way they deceived people, by misusing and misrepresenting spiritual gifts, is the same way Hell will misrepresent God's power to deceive them. 2 Corinthians 11:15 warns that they will meet their end "according to their works." As their false miracles and false prophecies led many people away from the truth, Hell's "powers" will do the same to them. That is why he will fulfill all the makings of a false prophet (cf. Deut. 13:15, Rev. 20:10).

Those who accept him as Christ will stand on one side of the spiritual rift. They will become the prophetic fallen who will be severed from the Church (Matt. 24:23, Mark 13:21). On the other side are those who will heed apocalyptic warnings. They will deny that the false prophet is Christ and be at odds with their former brothers and sisters in faith (Matt. 10:21–22). For them, the tribulation will become an enduring test of faith.

God said, "he that endureth [tribulation] to the end shall be saved" (Matt. 10:22).[4] The need to endure indicates that there will be no immediate relief. That is also an indication that the Church should be preparing for a long and devastating spiritual war. Those who do look for immediate relief during that time will find themselves unknowingly aligned with evil.

***

God did provide the correct sequence of events that would precede his return (Matt. 24:5–31). He revealed that he would be at the right hand of his Father, in heaven, when Death and Hell were loosed on the earth. His opening of the sealed scrolls in Revelation chapter 6 confirms that sequence of events. Notice that after the fifth seal was opened, John observed the souls of Christians who were slain (verse 9). That observation was made after Death and Hell were already loosed with the previous four seals (verses 1–8). Those future martyrs (faithful Christians) were slain during the Great Tribulation for keeping their faith in the death, burial, and resurrection of Jesus Christ (Rev. 20:4). Only after those events will the Lord return.

A Deceptive Teaching

For those who believe in a pre-tribulation rapture, there are significant questions that should be asked. How can Christians go looking for a false Christ if they will be taken away before his appearance (Matt. 24:26)? How can Death prevail against the saints–for a time–if the Church is no longer present on the earth (Rev. 13:7)? How can some Christians fall away and believe a lie if they will not be here to be tested? Those are legitimate questions for followers of the pre-tribulation doctrine. They show how out of sync that teaching is with Scripture.

Understanding that the Church will enter the Great Tribulation should not lead to disappointment (cf. James 1:3). The rapture will occur. It is written right into the Apocalypse. It is only the timing of its occurrence that is being taught incorrectly. That incorrect teaching is one of the reasons the Lord warned that many would come in his name and deceive many.

That pre-tribulation teaching is unknowingly preparing many people to receive the first "light" they see. That is why many apocalyptic texts emphasize the timing of the false prophet's appearance. God does not want faithful Christians deceived by his appearance.

The Rapture

Notice that immediately after the Lord opens the sixth seal, John observes an innumerable multitude of people who suddenly appear in heaven (Rev. 7:9–12). Those are faithful Christians who were raptured into the presence of the Lord. How do we know? Verses 13 and 14 tell us that those people were taken right out of the Great Tribulation and made clean with the blood of the Lamb. They were taken in an instant (1 Cor. 15:52). Therefore, after the period of trial and tribulation, God will send his angels to gather the remaining elect (Matt. 24:31).

That means that even though faithful Christians will be persecuted during the trial, they will be spared from the wrath that God will unleash on the earth (Rev. 8). Notice how the trumpets and censors come directly from God, not the beast or false prophet. The unsaved and fallen will not be spared (Rev. 6:17). It needs to be said that when faithful Christians are taken away, they will never again suffer at the hands of evil.

Abraham's Bosom

On an interesting note, the end time rapture will not be the first. When the Lord descended into the earth, for three days and three nights, he took the Old Testament saints with him to heaven (cf. Luke 16:22, Matt. 12:40, 2 Cor. 12:2). They were the first to be redeemed. Those are the people John heard singing before the throne of God in the presence of the Lamb (Rev. 5:9).

Those saints waited inside the earth, in the paradise God prepared for them, because they were under the former covenant and the high priest had not yet entered the holy place (Heb. 9:11–12). When Jesus did enter that holy place, they rejoiced and John was allowed to provide a written account as evidence so the earthly Church would know that the high priest was in his place. The next rapture will occur *during* the tribulation. To the unfaithful and impatient, the Lord's return will be very unexpected (Matt. 24:50).

NOTES

1. Read Revelation 19:19-20 and Daniel 7:24-25 for comparisons between those two wars.

2. The following are some examples of Scripture that emphasize patience: Luke 21:19, Rom. 5:3, 2 Cor. 6:4, Col. 1:11, 1 Thess. 1:3, 2 Thess. 1:4, and James 1:3. Also note that the Lord gave his followers information not meant to be understood by unfaithful or ungodly people (cf. Matt. 13:11–16).

3. That is the same abomination that causes desolation referred to several times in Daniel (cf. Dan. 12:11).

4. The word "overcometh" is commonly used with the same meaning as endurance (cf. Rev. 21:7). Emphasis is placed on keeping faith and lasting to the end (cf. Matt. 24:13, Mark 13:13).

7. HELL THE LAMB

What other reason would cause people to say that Christ had returned unless they truly believed he was here on Earth (Matt. 24:23). Jesus warned in the following verse: "I am come in my Father's name, and ye receive me not: if another shall come in his own name, him ye will receive" (John 5:43).[1] That was a foretelling of the false prophet's reception by the deceived. That joyous reception is mentioned again in Matthew 24:23.

When those Christians wrongly identify Hell as Christ, it will be because he appears to be what they were waiting for. In other words, he will fit their criteria of what a messiah should be. That is another reason Hell appears as a beast with "two horns *like a lamb*" (Rev. 13:11). The true Lamb of God is his Son (John 1:29, Rev. 5:6). So, saying Hell is like a lamb points to his fraudulent representation of Christ. That symbolism also emphasizes that even though he appears like a lamb, he speaks like his god the dragon. That clue is significant because Hell will look right, but not sound right. His words will not match his appearance. If people listen closely to what he will say, they will know he is a liar (cf. John 8:44). The problem is that many of them will not listen. They will accept him based on his deceptive appearance.

Judging by Appearance

Would you have been able to identify God's servants if you lived during their lifetimes? Can you spot them today? Do you know how they will look and act? Servants of the Lord usually conflicted with the status quo and still do to this day (John 15:19). They are often misunderstood, falsely judged,

45

and defied. Elijah may have been considered an arrogant and pompous man by today's standards because he was outspoken and challenged the hierarchy of the religions of his time (1 Kings 18:21–40). Could you imagine his reception in this current age of political correctness?

What would you do if you saw a man standing in the water, wearing clothes made of animal hair, eating locusts, and dunking people in the water? Would you have felt inclined to listen to his words or walk away? That strange man was John the Baptist (Matt. 3:4). Gideon was the most insignificant person in his family, but God turned him into a great leader (Judges 6). David was just a child when he killed a massive Philistine soldier and changed the outcome of a war (1 Sam. 17:15–51). Jeremiah walked the streets with a yoke around his neck to emphasize prophecy (Jer. 27:2). The list of nonconformists goes on and on.

Christians read epic stories about great heroes and heroines of the Bible, but never really think how they would have received them. Scripture teaches to look beyond the outward appearances of people, situations, or things, and judge righteous judgment (John 7:24). Why? Because many ungodly people, who seem right on the outside, want to introduce doctrines that challenge Christian core beliefs (2 Pet. 2:1).

Protecting your Faith

A good rule of thumb is to think of your faith the same way a guard thinks of his post. He protects it with his life. Before anyone can pass, they are asked to provide certain passwords. If the passwords are incorrect, they cannot enter. Likewise, Christians should not let everyone claiming to represent God past their post. Beyond your post is a protected space. That space represents your faith in the death, burial, and resurrection of the Lord. The passwords for those who want to pass are found in 1 John 4:1–2.[2] In those verses, Christians were warned to verbally challenge the spirits of people who want to pass. They, in turn, are required to say, "Jesus Christ is come in the flesh" and is God. He is more than just a powerful servant or great prophet. He is part of the Holy Trinity. Anyone who says otherwise is a deceiver.

Consider this: at night a guard may or may not be able to see who wants to pass. In the darkness he can only rely on what he hears. Likewise, in the darkness of the coming tribulation, Christians should rely on the same. That is very important, because some infiltrators look and act just like good Christians. Many times they operate right alongside the elect.

Recall how weeds were *among* the wheat. Likewise, infiltrators are among good Christians.

In comparison, think about a guard who fails to challenge for the passwords. Instead, he lets in a soldier who has on the same uniform. His appearance was enough to gain entry into the guard's protected space. Later that day, the soldier poisons the water supply, causing many people to become sick and ineffective. A subsequent investigation reveals that the guard let in an enemy soldier who was wearing a stolen uniform. The enemy's appearance in a friendly uniform was enough to deceive the guard. Likewise, many evil servants display the Christian faith to deceive. That is why outward appearances should never be used to judge righteousness (2 Cor. 5:7).

Great power, high positions, academic degrees, and potent leadership qualities can be misleading. How many times, throughout Scripture, were the well-dressed hypocrites in powerful positions chastised (e.g. Matt. 23:27–33)? Christians cannot judge based on what they see. They have to discipline themselves to look beyond outward appearances and apply the test laid out in 1 John 4:1–6. If a person fails that test then they know their message is false, no matter how influential or powerful they may be.

The warning that Satan will *appear* as an angel of light is profound (2 Cor. 11:14). Many apocalyptic texts warn that Hell will deceive by outward signs and miracles (Rev. 19:20). The people who follow him will not head these warnings. They will be impressed with his flattery, power, and outward appearance (Dan. 11:32).

God has a habit of repeating his lessons. Notice what the final two faithful servants will be wearing as they give a last call to repentance—sackcloth (Rev. 11:3)! God will send those two servants to preach against Hell's false ministry dressed in raggedy sackcloth.[3]

Falling Away

1 Timothy 4:1 mentions a departure from the faith. That begs the question of how a Christian can fall away if they are a part of the blood covenant? Notice in Matthew 12:31–32 that all sins are forgiven, even blasphemy against Jesus Christ, but blasphemy against the Holy Spirit is never forgiven (cf. Rev. 13:1). That is why Hebrew 9:22 states, "almost all things." Hell's religious system will lead unfaithful Christians to commit blasphemy against the Holy Spirit. That is why faithful Christians were warned to stay away. The risk is far too great.

That passage also answers the question of whether or not Christians can lose their salvation. The answer is a resounding yes! Anyone who commits blasphemy against the Holy Spirit is lost forever. Names in the Book of Life can be removed and blasphemy is the reason why (Rev. 3:5).

When Christians accept Jesus Christ as their Lord and Savior, they are washed clean of all forgivable sins. From that point on, they are sealed until the day of redemption (Eph. 4:30). However, the offense of blasphemy against the Holy Spirit is not cleansed by that covenant. It cannot be washed away. Once committed, that sin guarantees the offender a place in hell. It is the one and only unforgiveable sin.

***

Faithful Christians will heed these warnings. They will not be deceived by the false prophet's appearance or his false teachings. In fact, they will glorify God by continuing to preach the resurrection. Unfortunately, that is also why many of them will be killed (Dan. 11:33). Both Daniel and John saw those future martyrs (Dan. 7:21, 7:25, Rev. 13:7). Those are real people who will become examples to the world. God will test that last generation. It will be a trial for all mankind (cf. 1 Pet. 1:7, 2 Thess. 2:11–12, Rev. 3:10).

NOTES

1. Cf. Dan. 11:37.

2. Cf. Rom. 10:9.

3. Cf. 2 Pet. 3:7–9.

8. THE IMAGE OF ABOMINATION

Jesus related the false prophet to the abomination Daniel saw in his vision (Matt. 24:15). Daniel saw that abomination standing in the holy place of a future temple. While there, he put an ungodly thing inside the holy place. That thing causes desolation. For that reason, it is also referred to as an abomination (Dan. 11:31). Therefore, the false prophet is an abomination and the thing he places inside the temple is also an abomination.

Those perspectives of Hell standing in the holy place provide insightful clues about his deceptive religious system. The key word here is deceptive. It is not going to be obvious. It must appear to be somewhat in–line with Judeo–Christian beliefs, because many unfaithful Christians are well versed in messianic prophecy. Considering that God is the one sending the delusion, it is safe to say that the deceptive religious system will be convincing. Not only that, since it has been used before many people will not question its authenticity.

The Holy Place

Exodus 26 provides instructions for the construction of the earthly tabernacle. Within that tabernacle was a place so holy that only one priest was allowed to stand in it. That was the place of the second veil. It was called "the holy place," where the mercy seat rested on the Ark of the Covenant. The priests of the tabernacle represented what Jesus, the Son of God, became.

The same way they entered that holy place to atone for the sins of their people (Exod. 30:10), Jesus entered the ultimate holy place to atone for the sins of all who believe in him and have not committed the unforgiveable sin (Rev. 5:6, Heb. 4:14). Therefore, the place behind the second veil represented the throne of God the Father.

The false prophet's religious system will turn people back to the tabernacle for salvation (cf. Acts 7:49). For that reason, he will cause its reconstruction. He will also put a representation of the Ark back behind the veil. That act of placement fulfills the "set up" of the abominable thing (Dan. 12:11). Daniel wrote the reason why: "He magnified himself even to the prince of the host [Jesus Christ], and by him the daily sacrifice was taken away, and the place of his sanctuary was cast down" (Dan. 8:11).

Christians are hosts for the prince of hosts. He covers them in his blood daily and dwells in them. That is why Christians plead the blood of the Lamb. He is their daily sacrifice. That is also why they pray for daily bread, and Jesus is the Bread of Life (cf. Matt. 6:32–35, Luke 11:3, 22:19). Hell, however, will teach people to turn away from that belief and return to tabernacle worship. That is why he is observed so many times removing the daily sacrifice and defying the prince of hosts (cf. Dan. 11:31).

That is also why, in Revelation 9:20, John saw people refusing to repent "of the works of their hands, that they should not worship devils, and idols of gold, and silver, and brass, and stone, and of wood." Compare those materials to the materials used to build the tabernacle in the Old Testament. Wood was used to build the Ark, stone was used for altars, and so on (Exod. 20:25, 25:10). The tabernacle was made out of very specific materials (Exod. 26). In Revelation 9:20, readers "see" similar materials being worshipped by the unrepentant. By compounding those clues about the construction materials and Daniel's visions of Hell standing in the holy place, one can reason that Hell will reinstitute tabernacle worship.[1]

To unfaithful Christians, his religious system will appear to be a complete, fulfilling, and legitimate way to righteousness, minus the most important part–the resurrection. That is the trap designed to root out hypocrites from the Church. Hell will turn their focus toward the tabernacle and away from the resurrection of Jesus Christ.[2] In doing so, he will lead evil servants away from the Church.

The institution of Hell's religious system is clearly a future event, because the people deceived by the tabernacle argued that they wielded gifts that only became available to the Church at Pentecost. It would not have been possible for those people to know the Lord's name or wield spiritual gifts prior to the Lord's ascension into heaven (e.g. John 14:26). Therefore, Hell's religious system will affect not only unbelievers but also

Christians in the Church. That is why the condemned believed they were working in the Lord's name (Matt. 7:21–23, Rev. 19:20–21).

The Fifth Cherub

The Devil understands the significance of the Ark because at one time he was a part of what it represented. On several occasions, when God revealed himself to his servants, they saw four beasts posted at the four corners of his throne (e.g. Rev. 4:6, 5:6–8). Ezekiel, also a prophet, wrote the following verses that shed light on yet a fifth beast:

> Thou sealest up the sum, full of wisdom, and perfect in beauty. Thou hast been in Eden the garden of God; every precious stone was thy covering, the sardius, topaz, and the diamond, the beryl, the onyx, and the jasper, the sapphire, the emerald, and the carbuncle, and gold: the workmanship of thy tabrets and of thy pipes was prepared in thee in the day that thou wast created. Thou art the anointed cherub that covereth; and I have set thee so: thou wast upon the holy mountain of God...(Ezek. 28:12–14).

From those verses we see that a fifth beast was not posted at the corners, but instead, covered it. That covering cherub is no longer observed at the throne because he was cast out. Note the past tense in the last verse. The cherubim were affixed to the Ark because it was meant to be an accurate representation of God's throne in heaven (Exod. 25:18–20).

The Image has a Voice

Both Ezekiel and John saw that fifth cherub fall (Ezek. 28:16, Rev. 12:7–9). Isaiah, yet another prophet, gave us his name: Lucifer (Isa. 14:12). In Revelations, that fifth cherub is symbolized as a dragon or devil (12:7). Isaiah's prophecy also revealed that it was Lucifer's desire to be God that led to his fall (Isa. 14:13–14). That desire is still there. It will be Lucifer's voice that will speak through the Ark, and the world will worship him thinking it to be God the Father.

That is why Hell speaks like a dragon (Rev. 13:11). He communicates with his dragon god in the holy place and conveys what he hears to the world. How convincing! In the presence of the high priest (Hell), the Ark will become active. That is what is meant when it is written that he will "give life unto the image of the beast" (Rev. 13:15). The Ark will become active in his presence, as the true Ark of the former covenant became active for the Levite high priests.

That is why in Revelation 13:6 he is observed blaspheming the tabernacle in heaven while standing in his false tabernacle on Earth. In the theocracy of the fourth kingdom, Lucifer will be god; Death will be king, falsely representing the other Comforter (cf. John 14:16); and Hell will be their high priest, leading the world astray (Rev. 13:15–16).

Blasphemy Incarnate

Death's identification with the other Comforter is why so many people will be condemned. He will be blasphemy incarnate (cf. John 14:26). That is why in Revelation chapter 13 he is "highlighted" with blasphemy all over his heads and horns. That symbolism is a warning for what he represents. He will impersonate the Holy Spirit. Those who affiliate with him or his kingdom will have committed the unforgiveable sin (Matt. 12:31–32, Rev. 14:9–12). The promise to send the Comforter was already fulfilled at Pentecost (John 14:16, 14:26, 16:7, Rev. 5:6, Acts 2). The first beast, however, will present himself as the fulfillment of that prophecy, and because of his great power many will accept him or submit to his authority.

Think how much of an affront to God it will be to see a return to tabernacle worship after he tore the temple veils and glorified his son Jesus Christ (cf. Heb. 8:6, Heb. 9, Matt. 27:51).[3] God will never again dwell behind a veil (cf. Heb. 9). He dwells inside of every believer (Matt. 27:51). Christians host him in their bodies and for that reason he is the Lord of hosts. Without the cleansing blood of Jesus, many will be left desolate.

By re-educating the weak in faith, Hell will, in effect, teach that he (Jesus) was not the Son of God, but just a servant and prophet—hence the term "false prophet." If you think about it, who else could better explain away the death, burial, and resurrection than "Jesus" (cf. Dan. 7:25)? Instead of believing in the cleansing blood of the Lamb, unfaithful Christians will leave their first beliefs and entrust their salvation to a fraud and his tabernacle.[4] Think how much of an abomination it will be for God to see people washed clean in his blood turning their backs on him and looking to a demonic tabernacle for salvation (cf. Rom. 10:3, 2 Cor. 2:11).

Those who are aware of this coming false ministry will keep their faith and preach against it. They will refuse to reject their core beliefs (Dan. 11:31–33, Rev. 20:4). That is why many of them will suffer and die during that time (Rev. 6:9). The good news is that they will be raised again in glory. They will inhabit the true tabernacle that is now occupied by the real high priest (Heb. 8:1–2, 9:11–12).

Ungodly Faith

It will be a strange phenomenon but fallen Christians will suddenly develop a strongly rooted faith in the false prophet's lies. No matter what happens around them, they will not renounce his religion. They wield the gift of healing, but find themselves covered in sores (Rev. 16:11). They stand in the kingdom of their god, but are attacked by strange devilish bugs (Rev. 9:3–5). The god they worship cannot even explain why disasters continually torment his kingdom. Nothing fits the promised expectations of life with the Lord, but they never question the false prophet's authenticity. They are so devoted to his teachings that they will continue to commit blasphemy at the false tabernacle (cf. Rev. 9:20–21).

Throne Room Salutations

When Jesus was nailed to the cross he cried out "My God, my God, why hast thou forsaken me" (Mark 15:34). His cry acknowledged God the Father and God the Holy Spirit. Jesus is the third part of the Holy Trinity, so he only needed to acknowledge the other two. In comparison, take note of how the four remaining beasts around God's throne acknowledge the Holy Trinity. They say, "Holy, holy, holy, Lord God Almighty…" (Rev. 4:8). Holy is said three times to acknowledge the Father, Son, and Holy Spirit. All three are God and worthy of worship.

When those fallen Christians stand in judgment before the true Jesus Christ, they will be so deceived into thinking that he was just a prophet that they will say "Lord, Lord" and not acknowledge him as the third part of the Holy Trinity (Rev. 5:12–14). They will forget that Jesus is God (Heb. 1:1–4). Hell will have completely wiped the truth from their minds.

They will be so deceived into thinking that their tabernacle worship was the way to righteousness that they will actually complain to the all knowing and omnipresent Creator of all things (Matt. 8:12, 13:42). Notice how they never mention the blood covenant in their complaints. They only mention their works and what was most important to them: their ability to demonstrate spiritual gifts (Eph. 2:8–9). They brag about their outward signs of power and cry out "Lord, Lord!"

That faithless call is how many of them were grafted into the blood covenant in the first place (Acts 2:21). Even their spiritual predecessors used the name of the Lord in vain. This time, however, the Lord's name will not save them. They are the final generation of "weeds" that entangled themselves in the Church. The Lord's name meant nothing more to them than a brand to identify their clique and market their products. They called on a name that God exalted above all principalities and powers to feed nothing more than greed and self-gratification.

If they had the sincere desire to lay their sins at the Lord's feet, they would not be able to turn their backs on his resurrection. They would know that without the cleansing blood of his sacrifice there is no hope. The names of those former members of the Church will be removed from the Lamb's Book of Life (cf. Matt. 24:50–51, Rev. 3:5).

***

It should be said that cowards will share their fate. Cowards will not trust the message of the gospel. They will be more concerned about protecting their lives than standing up for truth (Matt. 16:25). They knew the truth but feared Death and Hell more than God (cf. Matt. 10:28, 2 Tim. 2:12). In Revelation 21:8 they are called the fearful.

Discernment and Deception

It is important to understand that Christians are not exempt from deception. Some churches are teaching that once a person is saved and filled with the Holy Spirit they are far removed from temptation. Remember in an earlier chapter that Satan was able to tempt the living Word of God. To assume that Christians are exempt because they are filled with the Holy Spirit creates a false sense of security (cf. Eph. 6:12–18). They will wrestle with temptation until they are literally made new in a physical sense (cf. Matt. 26:41, 1 Cor. 15:50–54).

To clarify, there is a spiritual renewal that takes place when saved and a physical renewal that will take place when the Lord returns. For now, the Church has to remain vigilant and guard against temptation (cf. 1 Pet.

5:8). Also keep in mind that God is not divided against himself (cf. Matt. 12:25–28). If he authorizes temptation or tribulation to test the faith of a Christian, then discernment will not work. Temptation can happen and will happen in the future. The problem is that a failing result during the Great Tribulation will be far worse than mere backsliding now. It will result in the actual loss of salvation.

NOTES

1. Hebrews chapters 9 and 10 provide excellent reasons and comparisons for the earthly tabernacle, but the time for its purpose has passed (see also Hebrews 8:1–2). Also note that the next tabernacle, which will far exceed any current expectations, will not be made with human hands (Heb. 9:11).

2. Cf. 1 Cor. 15:1–22.

3. Cf. Rev. 21:22.

4. The term "first faith" is used in 1 Tim. 5:12.

9. THE BROKEN COVENANT

In order for the false prophet to continue his ruse as the messiah, he will have to fulfill other important messianic prophecies. If not, his actions will not have any meaning for skeptical onlookers. That is why, in Daniel 9:27, the events are significant and recognizable by the Church.

One of those events is the confirmation of a covenant. The reason it is confirmed is because it is already well known but not yet fulfilled. The false prophet simply steps in and confirms it. The fact that it is confirmed for a short time indicates that it will only last long enough to deceive.

It is during that covenant that many impatient and unfaithful Christians will identify with him and go to him. Considering that he will have already fulfilled one important expectation by defeating the three warring kings, his resulting land covenant will further substantiate their perception of him as the messiah. Of course the land covenant was never his to fulfill in the first place, but its initial appearance of fulfillment will deceive many people. That is why they will go looking for him (Matt. 24:26). That, in and of itself, is a discrepancy because faithful servants will not have to go looking for the Lord. He will send his angels to gather them from wherever they are in the world (Matt. 24:27).

Israel's Hope

The false prophet's appearance of love for Israel is nothing more than a lie to draw people to him. As soon as he achieves that purpose, he will use his authority to merge Israel's territories into the fourth kingdom. In doing so, he will break the very covenant that deceived so many people.

That is why his appearance coincides with Death's final horse (Rev. 6:8). His land merger marks the final stages of God's trap.

Fortunately for Israel, God left a failsafe. Many of them will accept the false prophet during the "fulfillment" of the land covenant; however, when it is broken they will rebel. Remember God's warning about the unforgiveable sin (Matt. 12:31). Within that same passage is Israel's hope. Many will commit blasphemy against the Lord Jesus Christ, but even that sin is forgivable. They will not, however, accept Death's authority over their land. In denying him, they will not commit the unforgiveable sin (Matt. 12:31–32). That is one of the reasons Israel can and will be saved (Rom. 11:26). It is also why they will suffer alongside the Church (Mark 13:9).

On the other hand, many people will go to the next step. They will accept the authority of Death and become citizens of the fourth kingdom. Within that kingdom, they will need legal means to conduct trade, travel, and identify fellow citizens. Those legal means, referred to as marks, will be necessary for daily life. No one will be able to buy or sell without proper documentation showing that they are authorized to do so (Rev. 13:17).

The problem is that no matter how people affiliate with the fourth kingdom, they will have committed blasphemy against the Holy Spirit. Death and everything about him is blasphemy. That is why even his subordinate kings (horns) were "highlighted" with blasphemy (Rev. 13:1).

A Realistic Look at the Marks

There is a growing consensus that the marks of the beast will be technology based. With that in mind, consider the impact severe storms have on power grids and other basic utilities. It does not take much to disrupt technology for lengthy periods of time. Now, consider that during the Great Tribulation mountains will be moved out of their places and fire will fall from heaven. Even the Mount of Olives will be split in two, with both parts continually moving away from each other (Zech. 14:4). Isaiah 14:12–17 goes so far as to say that the world will be reduced to a wilderness (cf. 1 Thess. 5:3).

Those predictions point to devastating disasters that will be unlike any since before time. That is why technology-based marks are not very realistic. Plus, the make up of the marks is not what is important. Satan has no need for manmade technology. What is important is what they represent.

Keep in mind that the people who accept the marks will be deceived. To them, they will simply be acquiring the "tools" they will need to legally function in their kingdom. In their delusion they will not realize that the marks are an abomination to God. That is why faithful servants have to be mindful of what the marks represent and how they will be used to protect against deception.

A Warning about the Marks

The Great Tribulation will be a time of starvation, pestilence, wars, and drought. During that time, people may be tempted to accept help from citizens and authorities of a kingdom that is prospering. That is a grievous temptation that has to be avoided. Using any of the marks will result in damnation. They show that a person has been associated, in some way, with that blasphemous king. The irony of the matter is that the Lord's angels will use the marks to identify the fallen as citizens (children) of the false kingdom mentioned in Matthew 8:12. Those people will not be harvested with the Church (Matt. 13:28–30).

Matthew 8:11–12 seems very out of place, but read carefully and you will see that it contains apocalyptic information. The Lord was discussing a future time when people gathered from all around the world will fellowship with the patriarchs. He was comparing his true kingdom to the false kingdom of Death and Hell.

Practical uses of the Marks

The Numbers of Blasphemy:

Every president on United States currency has a number. George Washington's number is one because he is on the one dollar bill, Thomas Jefferson's number is two because he is on the two dollar bill, and so on. If George Washington's face were on all currency, he would have many numbers with his name. The number or *numbers* of the beast simply refer to the currency he will establish to prosper his economic block.[1] No one will be able to buy or sell without using his official currency.

The Name of Blasphemy:

Now picture an official document, such as a deed or marriage license. They are only valid because they bare an official government seal or authorized signature. The name of the beast is simply his seal or signature. You will not be able to conduct deeded transactions without official documents baring his seal, which according to the text will be his name.

The Marks of Blasphemy:

Keep in mind that Death is impersonating the Holy Spirit and Hell is impersonating the messiah. To keep up with that ruse they will need to seal citizens of their kingdom showing that they are "saved." That seal will be the primary form of identification between the authorities and citizens of the fourth kingdom. According to the text, the seal will be placed on the hands or foreheads of their followers (Rev. 13:16). In comparison, faithful servants will be sealed with the true name of God when he returns (Rev. 7:3, 3:12, 9:4, 14:1).

The Not So Little Horn

After the false prophet submits the kingdom of Israel to the first beast, he will still function as the high priest of the tabernacle. From that point forward, he will "exerciseth all the power of the first beast before him" that is to say, in his service (Rev. 13:12). That is why in Daniel's perspective he is observed serving in a lesser capacity—hence the term *little* horn (Dan. 7:8).

That lesser capacity is only in relation to the first beast because he is respected with fear and reverence, so much so that he is the one seen commanding all to worship the image of the beast upon penalty of death (Rev. 13:15). His stature is only less compared to the beast. To all others he is no little matter.

Hell's Notable Miracle

At some point during his reign, Death will be killed. John saw him "wounded to death" (Rev. 13:3). The world then bares witness to a miracle. He is resurrected, but by who? Who has power to raise the dead? Who called Lazarus from his tomb? It was Jesus the Son of God, but in this case it will be the false prophet. The remnants of the world will witness that miracle. For some, that will be more than enough to convince them that the false prophet is the messiah (cf. John 7:24, Rev. 13:12–14).

God set the parameters high for his test, because it will be difficult to weed out hypocrites. They know Scripture well and understand many of the same end time prophecies that faithful Christians understand. That is why the false prophet will be allowed to wield such great power. Of course, his power will not last forever, but for a time it will seem endless (cf. Rev. 19:20).

Ten Kingdoms

When the Lord returns and defeats the beast, the ten nations that rose to power during the tribulation will be judged and placed on probation (Rev. 20:3). [2] Another perspective confirms their probationary status (Dan. 7:11–12). Since that judgment follows the true advent of Christ, one can assume that those nations will exist during the millennial reign. The Lord will fulfill prophecy by making them his footstool (Matt. 22:44, Mark 12:36, Luke 20:43).

Zechariah chapter 14 provides even more details about those nations. In that perspective, the nations of the world wage war with Jerusalem (verse 2). That perspective is in–line with the war mentioned in Revelation chapter 19, where the Lord wars with the kings of the earth. Also note the plural in Revelation 17:14, because there is more than one. That is another disparity with the preterist viewpoint. There was only one nation at war with Jerusalem during the first century invasion, so it does not fit.

In all accounts of the war, the true Jesus Christ visibly intervenes. That is to say, he is literally here on the earth, with the armies of heaven, at war with those ten nations (Zech. 14:5). The aftermath of that war will be the subjugation of the entire world under the authority of Jesus Christ, his Father God, and the true Holy Spirit.

Just to be clear, those nations will be conquered. As such, the Lord will not view them in a positive light. They are his enemies and the enemies of his people—Christians and Jews alike. That is why in Zechariah 14:16–17 there is a penalty for any nation that does not observe the Feast of Tabernacles (cf. Rev. 21:26–27). That is a term of their probation. That is what is meant when it is written that he will rule with a rod of iron (Rev. 2:27). The Lord will have no need to rule his faithful servants with a rod of iron (cf. 1 Cor. 6:19–20, 12:12–13). They are his people and do his will

63

(cf. Matt. 7:21). The outer lands, however, will be subjugated to the Lord by force.

***

After his one thousand year reign on this earth, the Lord will release the devil to test those nations again. In their delusion, they will believe they can undo their defeat by warring with God's people again. In doing so they will violate their merciful probation. This time, however, the Lord will not grant them mercy. He will destroy them with a rain of fire and remove his kingdom to a new and better earth (Rev. 20:7–9, 21:1). This earth will pass away (2 Pet. 3:12–13).

NOTES

1. It is prophetic that the fourth kingdom will prosper (Dan. 8:24). The need to share in that prosperity may be one of the reasons Hell breaks his false version of the land covenant.

2. Their status will be comparable to probation before judgment. In other words, their penalty will be suspended while they meet the terms of their probation.

accepting as true what
is false

10. FAITH IN THE
COMING STORM

T here are many teachings about the end of time that have been
spread by ungodly people. Those teachings point to a fearful
and horrible end of the world. Some people have even tried to
predict the exact date of that destruction. Those false teachings contradict
Scripture, because the Lord said no one knows when those events will take
place (Mark 13:32). Christian teachings that follow suit misunderstand
end time prophecies. The Great Tribulation only marks the end for the
wicked. The saved will continue into eternity.

Spreading fear about the future is only meant to distract from the
truth. It is a part of the delusion (e.g. Matt. 24:11). The people who are
deceived by that delusion will accept spirits of fear and search for hope
in all the wrong places.[1] On the other hand, Christians who understand
the gift of apocalyptic texts will turn inward and rely on their faith, while
waiting patiently for the Lord. They will know that the coming tribulation
is just a test of faith for one brief moment in time.[2] 1 Peter 1:7–9 states:

> That the trial of your faith, being much more precious than of gold
> that perisheth, though it be tried with fire, might be found unto praise
> and honour and glory at the appearing of Jesus Christ: Whom having
> not seen, ye love; in whom, though now ye see him not, yet believing,
> ye rejoice with joy unspeakable and full of glory: Receiving the end of
> your faith, even the salvation of your souls.

Those verses sum up the tribulation strategy. That strategy is to live
by faith.[3] That was Job's example. Christians should never doubt what

Jesus accomplished on the cross.[4] His resurrection was their resurrection. He already stands in the holy place, where no man has ever set foot, and has made a place for his faithful servants if they will only believe and endure.

***

When the cleansing of the Church is complete, God will quiet the events of the tribulation the same way he quieted the storm that tested the apostles. Those same events that caused fear and panic will be quieted in an instant. Even the dreadful beast and his armies will be brought low to bow before the Lord (cf. Isa. 14:15–16, Ezek. 28:18–19). God is always in control. At no time will anything happen without his direct authorization. That is why the Church should not focus solely on the confusing "smoke and mirrors" of the tribulation. Those things were masterfully designed to lay the foundations for the test.

Unfortunately, many churches are already focusing on that confusion (cf. 2 Tim. 2:3–4). Their teachings are directing people's attention toward names, dates, and locations–but what is really important? In the storm that rocked the apostles' boat, Jesus asked, "how is it that ye have no faith" (Mark 4:40)? Instead of focusing on the "storm," faithful servants should be preparing to endure the test and defend the foundations of the Christian faith. The confusing events of the tribulation are not meant for them. That is why God provided apocalyptic warnings to see right through them. If during the tribulation he wants faithful Christians to be mindful of–but not caught up in–the confusion, why focus on it now?

The tribulation is just a filter to cleanse the Church. It is a rooting out process for those who called the Lord's name but never truly loved him or understood what he did for them (cf. 2 Thess. 2:10). An appreciation for his saving grace was never firmly rooted in their hearts. Christianity was just a religion to try while convenient. When God makes it inconvenient they will leave (Mark 4:17, 2 Tim. 4:3–7). That is why the most important thing for faithful Christians to focus on, and preach, is the death, burial, and resurrection of the Lord Jesus Christ. They should never accept compromise or other ways to righteousness. Faith in his resurrection is what God will look for when he returns (Luke 18:8).[5]

Even now, some Christians question his accomplishments. Many have already left the faith for other religions or hybrid versions of Christianity. In most cases, those new beliefs focus on various forms of works (Eph.

2:8–9). None of them provide answers for humanity's sinful nature. Only faith in what Jesus accomplished at the cross can address that sin.

The Travail of Birth Pains

The Lord compared the end time tribulation to birth pains. Much like birth pains, when it ends there will be a new and glorious life (John 16:19–22, 1 Thess. 5:3). Another parallel that can be drawn from that comparison is how a pregnant woman prepares to receive her child. She knows that there will be pain and suffering when her gestation period ends, but looks right past it to the wonderful life she will help bring into the world. No one can see her baby, but she knows he is there. She knows that soon he will be seen and she will share her life with him.

During the birth pains of the Great Tribulation, faithful Christians will feel oppressed by evil. They will hear lies about their Lord. Many will be cut off from friends and family. Regardless, they know God is there. Only in the end will they see their Savior and enjoy their wonderful new life in his kingdom. That is the patience of the saints.

"Fight the good fight of faith"
1 Timothy 6:12

NOTES

1. Cf. 2 Tim. 1:7.

2. Cf. Matt. 10:22, Rom. 5:3–4.

3. Cf. Rom. 1:17.

4. Cf. Rom. 8:24–25.

5. That question about finding faith points to his test.

APPENDIX A:
AFFIRMATION OF FAITH

Lord, I know that you are the Son of the living God who died on a cross for me. I believe that you rose on the third day and conquered death. You are the Lamb of God. As such, you already entered the tabernacle in heaven and stood in the holy place as the ultimate sacrifice for my sins. There is no other way to righteousness because you left nothing undone. Belief in your sacrifice is the only way to heaven.

I know that this world is a proving ground for your faithful servants. I pray that you continually strengthen my faith in your accomplishments and form me into a better and more confident servant. I trust in you, Lord, and I will wait patiently for your return. Remember me in your kingdom and keep a place for me. In the name of Jesus Christ, my Lord and Savior, I pray, Amen.

FIGURE 1: Progression of events for the unfaithful

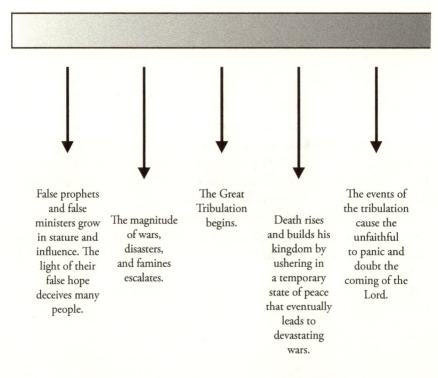

False prophets and false ministers grow in stature and influence. The light of their false hope deceives many people.

The magnitude of wars, disasters, and famines escalates.

The Great Tribulation begins.

Death rises and builds his kingdom by ushering in a temporary state of peace that eventually leads to devastating wars.

The events of the tribulation cause the unfaithful to panic and doubt the coming of the Lord.

Hell rises to power at the height of their doubts and is accepted as their messiah.

Hell directs the unfaithful to his tabernacle for salvation.

Hell submits Israel and all the deceived under the authority of Death and causes all people to receive marks of the fourth kingdom.

The true Lord returns and condemns them all to the lake of fire.

FIGURE 2: Progression of events for the faithful

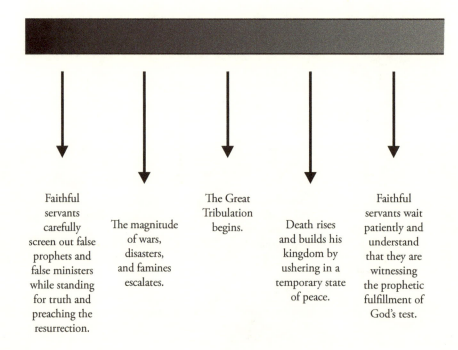

Faithful servants carefully screen out false prophets and false ministers while standing for truth and preaching the resurrection.

The magnitude of wars, disasters, and famines escalates.

The Great Tribulation begins.

Death rises and builds his kingdom by ushering in a temporary state of peace.

Faithful servants wait patiently and understand that they are witnessing the prophetic fulfillment of God's test.

They endure countless hardships for keeping faith in the resurrection.

They hear rumors that the messiah returned, but refuse to acknowledge him or go looking for him, because they know he is a fraud.

They are snatched away to heaven while God's furry is unleashed on the earth.

They return to Earth with the Lord and rule with him for one thousand years.

APPENDIX B:
THE FIRST AND SECOND DAMNATION

The assertion that the end time tribulation will cleanse the Church is supported by the distinction between the first and second resurrections (cf. John 5:28–29, Acts 24:15). Notice how only the dead in Christ experience the "resurrection of life" (John 5:29, Rev. 20:4–6). The unsaved dead, however, will not be resurrected until the millennial reign ends. That second resurrection, at the end of the millennial reign, substantiates the viewpoint that only evil servants will be condemned at the beginning of the millennial reign (Matt. 13:41–43).

To clarify, the unsaved nations found alive when the Lord returns will be allowed to continue living during the millennial reign (Dan. 7:11–12). They will exist as defeated foes until the devil is released to test them again. Ultimately, they will fail that test and attempt to rise against the kingdom of God. That violation of probation will result in a rain of fire that will completely wipe them out (Rev. 20:7–9). At that point, no unsaved person will be alive on Earth. That is when the "resurrection of damnation" will take place (John 5:29).

Keep in mind that evil servants were cast into the lake of fire at the beginning of the millennial reign (Rev. 19:20). They are the symbolic tares that were gathered and burned before the Church was gathered into the Lord's kingdom (Matt. 13:30, 13:42). That is why the post–millennial second resurrection, and resulting damnation, cannot be for evil servants. They will already be in the lake of fire. Therefore, the second resurrection has to be for every unsaved man and woman whoever lived (Rev. 20:9–15).

Those people will *join* evil servants in the lake of fire (Rev. 20:10). That is why the term "second death" is used to describe their fate (Rev. 20:14).

For evil servants, the lake of fire will be their first experience with death. That is because they are cast alive into the lake of fire, where they will remain forever (Matt. 13:30, 13:41–43). Likewise, the beast and false prophet will share their fate (Rev. 19:20). On the other hand, people who died in sin, throughout history, including those killed in the rain of fire, must be raised again to face death for a second time–hence the term "second death." Until that time, their souls will remain in the depths of hell (cf. Psalm 63:9, Eph. 4:9, Isa. 14:15, Luke 16:22).

APPENDIX C:
CAN CHRISTIANS JUDGE?

The question of whether or not Christians can judge has sparked debate for a very long time. Arguably, the problem is that certain verses dealing with judgment have been incorrectly applied to the Church without regard for the intended audience. It is important to identify the intended audience and then understand what that audience heard.[1] It is also important not to apply every verse in Scripture to the Church unless it was expressly conveyed in the New Covenant (Heb. 8:6, 2 Cor. 3).[2]

Some things were directed at the Church and some things were not. For example, Matthew 7:1 was clearly directed at hypocrites. Those were sinful people, acting holy, described as dogs and false prophets (Matt. 7:6, 7:15). Compare that to Romans 2:1 where Paul states, "thou that judgest doest the same things [as the accused]." His point was that hypocrites should not judge because they were in no position to judge (2 Pet. 2:20–22). Hypocrisy prevents a person from being able to judge righteously (John 7:24). That is why the source of the hypocrisy must be removed first. Notice how once the beam (hypocrisy) is removed focus can then be shifted to another (Matt. 7:5). Therefore, it is not faithful Christians who should not judge, only religious hypocrites. In fact, Matthew 7:1–5 was directed solely at hypocrites–not the faithful Church!

Consider this, when Paul found Christians suing each other in secular courts he asked "are ye unworthy to judge the smallest matters" (1 Cor. 6:1–11)? In other words, *judge* among yourselves and do not send Christian brothers and sisters before the unsaved in secular courts. Those verses were specifically directed at faithful Christians and therefore convey in the New

Covenant. Of course, when faithful Christians try to judge, or express opinions, they are quickly silenced and referred to verses like Romans 14:13. Even unbelievers cite Scripture to silence the Church. The problem is that those verses are often misunderstood.

Romans 14:13, for example, was directed specifically at Christian Jews who had points of disagreement with Christian Gentiles (Rom. 14:1–23). That is why throughout Romans there is a general overtone of unification. That is also why there is a comparison of the different habits practiced by both groups (e.g. Rom. 14:5–6). Paul was teaching Christian Jews and Christian Gentiles to be one in Christ. He did not want rituals to place stumbling blocks in front of the unified body of Christ (verse 13). Also notice the word "brother" in verse 13. Paul saw both sects as brothers in the body of Christ. Romans 14:13 was never meant to silence the Christian Church.

Imagine if Christians became politically correct and failed to rebuke sin (1 Tim. 5:20). Imagine if they never corrected each other or questioned doctrines. Christians are already pressured to compromise and keep their beliefs a secret, but the Lord said to spread the good news to the ends of the earth (e.g. Mark 16:15). Political correctness and Christianity will never go hand in hand (Luke 6:22-23, John 15:18).

NOTES

1. Gordon D. Fee and Douglas Stuart, *How to Read the Bible for all its Worth*. Grand Rapids: Zondervan, 2003. See pages 23.

2. Ibid., 167.

SELECTED BIBLIOGRAPHY

Bible: TNIV. *Today's New International Version: Study Bible.* Grand Rapids: Zondervan, 2006.

Edward J. Young. *The Prophecy of Daniel* (Grand Rapids: Eerdmans, 1949), 208. Mentioned in Stephen R. Miller, *The New American Commentary: Daniel*, Vol. 18. (Nashville: B&H, 1994), 270.

Fee, Gordon D., and Douglas Stuart. *How to Read the Bible for all its worth.* (3rd ed.). Grand Rapids, MI: Zondervan, 2003.

Gentry, Kenneth L., Sam Hamstra Jr., C. Marvin Pate, and Robert L. Thomas. *Four Views on the Book of Revelation.* Edited by Stanley Gundry and C. Marvin Pate. Grand Rapids: Zondervan, 1998.

Harbin, Michael A. *The Promise and the Blessing: A Historical Survey of the Old and New Testaments.* Grand Rapids: Zondervan, 2005.

Keener, Craig S. *The NIV Application Commentary: Revelation.* Grand Rapids: Zondervan, 2000.

Longman III, Tremper. *The NIV Application Commentary: Daniel.* Grand Rapids: Zondervan, 1999.

MacLeod, David J. "The Fourth 'Last Thing': The Millennial Kingdom of Christ (Rev. 20:4–6)," *Bibliotheca Sacra 157* (Jan., 2000): 44–67 (esp. 50–51).

Mayhue, Richard L. "Jesus: A Preterist or Futurist?" in *The Master's Seminary Journal* 14:1 (Spring, 2003), 9–22.

Miller, Stephen R. *The New American Commentary* (Vol. 18). Nashville: Broadman & Holman, 1994.

Poythress, Vern. "Genre and Hermeneutics in Rev. 20:1–6," *Journal of the Evangelical Theological Society 36* (March 1993). 41–54.

NOTES

CPSIA information can be obtained
at www.ICGtesting.com
Printed in the USA
BVHW041039180523
664420BV00004B/48